THOUGHTS ON HOLY COMMUNION

THOUGHTS ON HOLY COMMUNION

by

J. ERNEST RATTENBURY

O that all men would haste
To the spiritual feast,
At Jesus's word
Do this, *and be fed with the love of our Lord!*

LONDON
THE EPWORTH PRESS

FIRST PUBLISHED IN 1958

© THE EPWORTH PRESS 1958

Book Steward
FRANK H. CUMBERS

SET IN MONOTYPE BASKERVILLE AND PRINTED IN
GREAT BRITAIN BY THE CAMELOT PRESS LTD
LONDON AND SOUTHAMPTON

Contents

CHAPTER ONE

Introduction

I

THE FOLLOWING pages are not a systematic treatise on the doctrine of Holy Communion; they are the personal reflections of one who has come to regard this devotion as the most evangelical service of the Christian Church, and are written for the general reader. My background is evangelical, indeed intensely evangelistic. We cherished in our family a great tradition of evangelical revivalism, and to that evangelical training I owe an immeasurable debt. My parents' deep concern was to get people converted. They believed, as I believe, that the justification of Methodism as a separate religious organization is its fervent evangelism. No words were more familiar in my home than the line in Charles Wesley's hymn: 'O let me commend my Saviour to you.'

My people were not anti-sacramentalists, and although Holy Communion in Methodism in those days was infrequently celebrated, it was regarded as a commandment of Jesus to be obeyed. The Wesleyan doctrine of the real presence was always taught, though I remember that when I asked what was the difference between the presence of our Saviour in Holy Communion and at other times, the answer, 'a *special* presence', rather baffled me. But it is true that Holy Communion was in practice treated as of subordinate importance.

Methodists possess a great eucharistic tradition. Indeed it is not improper to describe the Evangelical Revival as also a sacramental revival. Sacramental observance in the eighteenth century was normally very slight in the Church of England. There is no parallel in its history with the enormous crowds of early Methodists which thronged the churches and embarrassed the clergy by their numbers at Holy Communion. John

Wesley records many services where hundreds of people communicated; sometimes the number was over a thousand—in one place thirteen hundred, and in another seventeen hundred, and so on—and be it noted that the crowds were never greater than at the height of the revival. The importance of this devotion is emphasized by the fact that within the first decade of the revival Charles Wesley wrote his *Hymns on the Lord's Supper*, 166 in number.

In the nineteenth century, for many reasons, sacramental devotion in Methodism languished. This was partly due to what John Wesley once called 'an overgrown fear of Popery'.[1] This fear was occasioned by the many controversies resulting from the Oxford Movement. Round about 1870 there was considerable controversy between Anglo-Catholics and Methodists on the Wesleyan doctrine. The Methodists defended their lessened sacramentalism by minimizing, unjustifiably, the teaching and practice of the Wesleys. The Anglicans exaggerated Wesley's Anglican teaching, and failed to see it in proportion to his evangelical mission.[2]

At the present time the sacramental devotions are probably more observed by Methodists than they have been since the earliest days, but there is still much to be done. In many cases there is a lurking suspicion that sacramentalism is somehow inconsistent with evangelism. There is a dread, not altogether unhealthy, of ceremonialism and ritualism; what is needed, people tell us, is the simple Gospel. There is a failure still to realize that the Eucharist preaches the Gospel. Many are puzzled by the emphasis put on eucharistic worship. There is a lamentable lack of instruction on this important subject. Methodist literature on the subject since the publication of Wesley's eucharistic hymns is very small. As a consequence many people fail to gain the deep spiritual benefits that come from eucharistic worship.

The general literature of eucharistic worship is enormous in bulk, and is generally difficult, because of its technical character,

[1] See J. E. Rattenbury, *The Eucharistic Hymns of John and Charles Wesley*, pp. 148ff.
[2] Ibid.

for any but students to read. In modern times the research of scholars has greatly increased our knowledge, and numerous works, historical and critical, have resulted in this and other countries. But there seems to be a lack of a simple, short and readable book which deals with the history and meaning of Holy Communion. An attempt will be made in the following pages to meet that want. Perhaps I may be excused for writing a sentence or two about my personal relations to this subject.

I often used to hear, when a youth, a statement which at that time impressed me. The assertion was made that evangelicalism and sacramentalism were opposed to each other and one must take one's choice between these two alternatives. But in my early ministry I accidentally came across a hymn by Charles Wesley, I think in a pamphlet (the 166th of his *Hymns on the Lord's Supper*), which attributed the decay of religion to neglect of Holy Communion. At that time I did not know of the existence of this hymn-book, and was amazed at such descriptions of the early Christians as the following:

> *From house to house they broke the bread*
> *Impregnated with life Divine,*
> *And drank the Spirit of their Head*
> *Transmitted in the sacred wine.*

I was amazed that Charles Wesley should attribute the decline of religious zeal to the loss of daily communion:

> *Why is the faithful seed decreased,*
> *The life of God extinct and dead?*
> *The daily sacrifice is ceased,*
> *And charity to heaven is fled.*

How could such extreme sacramentalism be harmonized with the evangelism of Charles Wesley at the period of his most fervent evangelical preaching? I did not understand, but it set me thinking. Through reading in the *Methodist Times* the fervent appeals of Hugh Price Hughes to Methodists, I found further confirmation of my suspicion that evangelicalism or sacramentalism was a false and misleading antithesis. In these appeals he wrote in the strongest language of the serious neglect by Methodists of Holy Communion. These words were written by one whom I knew to be one of the greatest evangelists of the time.

I myself later found in the practice of Holy Communion great help in the evangelistic work which was my chief employment for many years. During all my career as an evangelist, I practised and inculcated the observance of Holy Communion.

The subject is one about which I have written a good deal, and read as much as I could. As the following pages contain my personal conclusions on eucharistic practice and worship, I hope I may be pardoned for these autobiographical references which may explain to some why an evangelist has come to believe in the evangelical value of eucharistic worship.

II

It is difficult to write about the Eucharist without falling into controversy. Indeed it is probably true to say that no good man has ever made a statement about Holy Communion which has not been contradicted by some other good man. The purpose of this book, however, is devotional, and controversial statements will be avoided as much as possible. The term '*sacramentum unitatis*', when one considers the fact that it has been the subject of so much controversy, may at first sight appear to be quite absurd, and yet how true it is. This sacrament, because of its universal observance, has been regarded by the overwhelming majority of Christian people in every century as the central devotion of the Christian Church. Here we find a unity of conviction joined with a great diversity of practice and opinion.

Whoever deals with this sacrament acknowledges some element of mystery in it, something that transcends reason and demands faith. Even Thomas Aquinas in his great hymn with his precise definitions writes:

> *Doth it pass thy comprehending?*
> *Yet by faith, thy sight transcending,*
> *Wondrous things are understood.*

> *Yea, beneath these signs are hidden*
> *Glorious things to sight forbidden:*
> *Look not on the outward sign.*

I cannot but feel that close definition of this mystery has been a mistake. Although it is true that we must use our God-given intelligence in attempting an understanding, there are mysteries that in the nature of the case are beyond our human comprehension, and for my part I feel the rhyme attributed, I think probably truly, to Queen Elizabeth I is the wisest statement that I know.

> *Christ was the Word that spake it;*
> *He took the bread and brake it;*
> *And what that word did make it,*
> *That I believe and take it.*

Surely such words as these can be spoken by all Christians. There is no reason why a Catholic, however much more he may believe, should not accept these words, and the Protestant can hardly fail to do so. These words of the great queen provide a basis of unity which is well worth universal adoption. Faith in Christ and in His word, even if we do not entirely understand the meaning of His word, even if there is a mystery that evades us, is essential.

It will be remembered that people forsook Jesus because they could not understand His teaching about the bread of life. We may well join with Peter in his response to the words of Jesus, 'Will ye also go away?'—'To whom should we go save unto Thee. Thou hast the words of eternal life.'

Brilioth complains of the way in which men seize a fragment of eucharistic truth and are blinded to its totality. The Eucharist is a gem of many facets; the brilliance of one of them seems to blind the eyes of those who rejoice in it to the fact that there are many others. Or to change the figure, we may compare it to the heavenly city with twelve gates, each of one pearl. The men who enter through the north gate, somewhat icily, must not ignore the gate on the sunny south of the city.

All the main truths of the Christian religion find their

expression in the symbols of the Lord's Supper. The truth of the incarnation and of the atoning love made manifest in the new covenant of the blood of Christ, the death of Christ proclaimed by every Eucharist until He comes, the fact that He lives for ever amongst us and that His presence makes the feast, the necessary penitence of heart and saving faith in the Saviour—these are some of the many facts which eucharistic faith and practice denote. But even so, we see through a glass darkly.

> *Author of life divine,*
> *Who hast a table spread,*
> *Furnished with mystic wine*
> *And everlasting bread,*
> *Preserve the life Thyself hast given,*
> *And feed and train us up for heaven.*
>
> *Our needy souls sustain*
> *With fresh supplies of love,*
> *Till all Thy life we gain,*
> *And all Thy fullness prove,*
> *And, strengthened by Thy perfect grace*
> *Behold without a veil Thy face.*[3]

III

The difficulty I found in my early days about the sacrament was its formality—indeed, if I may say so, its materialism. There is a well-known saying, paradoxical as usual, of G. K. Chesterton which is worth recording: 'I am a Christian because Christianity is the most materialistic of all religions.' I am sure this statement must have shocked many people, but is it not at least an important half-truth if not more? As with most people who have any Puritan background the emphasis of spiritual religion was very dominant in my youth. How could I forget such passages as 'God is a spirit, and they that worship Him must worship Him in spirit and in truth', 'The letter killeth, the spirit giveth life', and 'Walk not after the flesh, but after the spirit'? Some lingering effect of the ancient Christian heresy that matter is intrinsically evil was probably

[3] *MHB*, No. 764.

the cause of my feeling, but no believer in the incarnation of Christ can think that matter is evil. 'The word was made flesh, and we beheld His glory.' 'The earth is the Lord's, and the fullness thereof.' Material things are not of themselves evil, but good. The touch of Christ makes them sacred.

> *Love, joy and hope like flowers*
> *Spring in His path to birth.*

Often I used to wonder why it was that Jesus took clay to cure the blindness of a man. Why did He trouble about the five loaves and two fishes when He had five thousand people to feed? They would not have fed more than a dozen of the multitude, and so nearly five thousand were fed by nothing. Why did Jesus use the material things? And even a deeper question issues: Why was the manhood of Jesus necessary for man's salvation? Could not God have done without such a material thing as the human body? But 'Christianity', says Chesterton, 'is the most materialistic of religions'. The truth is that God uses material things as His instruments of spiritual life. That is the sacramental idea which has many and wide applications. Our Lord's use of bread and wine as material instruments of blessing and teaching entirely corresponds with what His incarnation involves. How wonderfully it fits into the human framework.

There are many common material things that are a means of spiritual blessing to all human beings. Material monuments, for instance, awaken spiritual thoughts of gratitude for great providence; but simpler than this, we all find in keepsakes material things that open for us flood-gates of memory and affection. I have known very unsentimental people who treasure pressed flowers because of the memories they evoke. Many women possess valuable gems, but treasure most some valueless trinket given to them by one who loved them. We all possess books, portraits, letters of no intrinsic value, but we treasure them because at some time or other they evoke the memory of experiences known only to ourselves, but deeply valued.

Nearly seventy years ago I heard a sermon, not from a

minister, but from a local preacher who was also a distinguished advocate in the criminal courts, and afterwards a judge. That sermon by Mr S. D. Waddy left an indelible impression on my memory, chiefly because of an illustration which he used. One day, he said, he was visiting a client, who was also a friend, in order to discuss a matter of business which concerned them both. When he entered the room he noticed that his friend was quickly putting away a sheet of writing-paper which appeared to be wet, but then his friend paused and said: 'You are a friend of mine. I will tell you what this paper is. It is the last letter that my mother ever wrote to me, and it congratulated me upon an early success and ended with words substantially these. "My dear boy, though I am very grateful for your success, do not forget your father's God. I would rather you were a Christian man than a successful one. God bless you." My mother died soon after this letter was written, and whenever in my business life I am puzzled as to what is the right action in this or that instance, I read my mother's letter and it helps me to do the right thing.' Here is an instance. How many are like it, of the way a material thing, a crumpled and tear-stained letter, can be the instrument of spiritual blessing.

Such material symbols as these play a large part in many lives, but the greatest of all material symbols are the broken piece of bread and the cup of wine, material things, which Jesus consecrated not only as a perpetual memory of Himself, but as instruments, when used by penitent and believing men, of the redeeming love with which He set men free.

CHAPTER TWO

The Last Supper

I

WE HAVE in the New Testament four accounts of the Last Supper. Two of them, St Mark's and St Matthew's, are substantially identical. St Paul's account in 1 Corinthians 11 is the earliest and fullest. It is the account which the Church has incorporated into the office of Holy Communion. St Luke's account, as it is written in our versions, differs from the others in the addition of a cup of wine distributed before Jesus took and blessed the bread. There seems, however, to be strong reason for the opinion that Luke's original account ended with the words, 'This is my body', and that the words, 'which is given for you: this do in remembrance of me. Likewise also the cup after supper, saying, This cup is the new testament in my blood, which is shed for you', were added by another hand to give a completer account of what really happened.[1] It must be remembered that none of these accounts was written by men who were present at the Last Supper. They received their information from others, and their informants varied in detail.[2] We must add their details together in order to acquire a true picture. Whether St Luke wrote the words himself is not so important as whether or not the words are true, and the evidence of the other accounts removes any reasonable doubt of their veracity. If the description of the Lord's Supper to be found later in this chapter is accepted,[3] the chief difficulty of the Lucan account vanishes.

St John's Gospel gives us no description of the Last Supper,

[1] Luke 22$^{19-20}$.

[2] The important fact of course is not the variation of the details, but the unanimous agreement on the essential facts of the words of Jesus about the bread and wine.

[3] See pp. 17-21.

though his description of the events of that memorable night are much fuller than those of the other evangelists, and will be found important when in a later chapter we consider the meaning of Communion. But in this chapter we shall deal with facts rather than meaning. There is one detail of fact in this Gospel, however, which is relevant to the Last Supper, namely the feet-washing of the disciples by Jesus, and this is recorded only by St John.

The most valuable of these accounts is that of St Paul, not only because of its earlier date, but because it shows how early problems arose in a Church of converted pagans, and how the apostle dealt with them. It is also important because, as is shown not only in the eleventh chapter of 1 Corinthians, but in the tenth, the teaching of St Paul must have had great influence on the understanding and development of eucharistic worship.

The accounts of St Mark and St Matthew suggest that the Last Supper was the Paschal feast of Jesus and His disciples. This suggestion is lacking in St John, and the date in St John is different from that in the synoptics. It is generally agreed (Jeremias is an exception) amongst scholars today that St John's dating must be followed. A good account of the reasons can be found in Nolloth.[4]

St Paul calls Christ 'our Passover'.[5] Does not this imply that, at the time that the Jews were preparing the Paschal lamb for the Paschal feast, the Lamb of God, our one perfect and sufficient sacrifice, was dying on the Cross.

If, then, the Last Supper was not the Paschal feast, was it anything more than the farewell supper of Jesus with His friends, at which He instituted Holy Communion? It has been thought by many critics that such a deliberate institution at that time is very unlikely, but modern research into Jewish customs has given (though this is not universally accepted by scholars at the present time) a natural, and I think conclusive, explanation of what happened. The Jews, even in their ordinary domestic meals, were very devout in their thanksgivings for food, and in their prayer books are to be found the

[4] *The Fourth Evangelist*, p. 118.   [5] 1 Corinthians 5⁷.

thanksgivings and prayers which they made. One thanksgiving was always rendered: 'Blessed be Thou, O Lord our God, eternal King, who bringest forth bread from the earth.' But at public meals there were naturally more formalities than at private ones.

Dom Gregory Dix writes: 'From what occurred at it and from the way in which it was regarded by the primitive Jewish Christian Church it is evident that the Last Supper was a Jewish "religious meal" of some kind. The type to which it best conforms is the formal supper of a *chabûrah* (plural *chabûrôth*, from *chaber*=a friend).

'These *chabûrôth* were little private groups or informal societies of friends banded together for purposes of special devotion and charity, existing within the ordinary Jewish congregations, much like the original "Methodist" societies within the Church of England before the breach with the Church authorities developed. More than one modern scholar, as well Jewish as Christian, has remarked that in Jewish eyes our Lord and His disciples would have formed just such a *chabûrah*, only distinguished from hundreds of other similar societies by its unusually close bond and by the exceptionally independent attitude of its leader towards the accepted religious authorities. The corporate meeting of a *chabûrah* regularly took the form of a weekly supper. . . . The purpose of the supper was chiefly mutual recreation and social intercourse, though the business of the society was also managed on these occasions. Given the special religious background of such a society, religious topics—of perpetual interest to all Jews—normally formed the staple subject of conversation of any such meal.'[6]

The prayers and blessings at Jewish meals, both private and public, are found in rabbinical books.[7]

The Chabûrah meal

No kind of food was partaken without preliminary giving of thanks. If relishes were served before the meal proper began (there might be up to three relishes) each guest said the

[6] *The Shape of the Liturgy*, pp. 50-1.
[7] The Jewish tractate *Berākhoth* (blessings); see *Shape of the Liturgy*, p. 51.

B

blessing for himself. Then they all washed their hands, reciting meanwhile a special benediction. After this point no late-comers might join the *chabûrah* meal, for the meal proper began with handwashing and 'grace before meals', and only those who shared in this might partake.

As in all Jewish meals, the host or leader took bread and broke it, with the appropriate blessing. He then partook of a fragment himself and gave a piece to each person at the table. The meal followed, the host giving thanks for each fresh kind of food brought to table. If wine were served, each person blessed his own wine-cup every time it was re-filled.

At the close of the meal an attendant brought round a basin and a napkin and hands were washed again. Finally came the 'Thanksgiving'. This was a long prayer said by the host in the name of all who had eaten of the meal. On an important family occasion, and at a *chabûrah* supper in particular, it was recited over a special cup of wine, known as the 'cup of blessing'. At the end of the 'Thanksgiving' this was sipped by whoever had recited the prayer, then handed round to each person to sip. Finally, at a *chabûrah* supper, the members sang a psalm, and then the meeting broke up.

'This, then, is the general Jewish background of the Last Supper, which the New Testament accounts presuppose almost at every word (especially is this true of that in 1 Corinthians 11). It is a *chabûrah* supper, such as our Lord and His disciples were accustomed to hold regularly, held on this occasion twenty-four hours before the passover of that year. It is a meal held with some little formality and ceremony because it has a religious significance of its own.'[8]

First come the relishes. Our Lord takes a cup of wine and declines to drink it Himself but tells the apostles to divide it amongst themselves because He will not drink 'of the fruit of the vine until the Kingdom of God shall come'.[9] These words of Jesus are associated by the other synoptists with the later cup. They may of course have been spoken then, but the fact that wine was drunk before the commencement of the supper

[8] The Jewish tractate *Berākhoth* (blessings); see *Shape of the Liturgy*, p. 54.
[9] Luke 22[17].

solves the principal difficulty of St Luke's account, namely the mention of a cup of wine before the supper as well as after it. These words of Jesus are of great importance, so much so that some scholars regard them as vital to an understanding of the Supper. While such interpretation seems a one-sided theory, the sense of anticipation of future triumph cannot be ignored and must have had meaning to the Apostles. Then, as at all *chabûrah* meals, comes the washing of hands and the usual grace. 'Our Lord takes bread and breaks it, just as He had always done before, just as every Jewish householder and every president of any *chabûrah* took it and broke it at every supper table in Israel throughout the year. He "gives thanks" over it, but the words of His Thanksgiving are not recorded. Of course not! Why should they be? Every Jewish child knew them by heart: "Blessed be Thou, O Lord our God, eternal King, who bringest forth bread from the earth." '[10] Then the pieces of bread broken from the loaf were distributed as they had been many times before and would be many times again at similar meals when Jesus was no longer with them. But before the distribution took place He spoke the words which, along with the similar words spoken later over the cup of blessing, turned the Jewish meal into the Christian Sacrament. These surprising and enigmatical words were: 'This is my body.' They applied to the fragments of bread broken from the loaf.

Of the details of the meal itself we have no record except concerning the sop which Jesus gave to Judas, who afterwards went out to betray his Master. Of his departure St John wrote his terse and terrible epitaph: 'And it was night.' A feature of the meal must have been the conversation and discussions between Jesus and His disciples. It is impossible to know exactly when these took place, but it seems probable that the discussion as to who was the greatest, recorded by St Luke (22[24]), took place during the meal and suggested the action of Jesus at its close. This action is described by Gregory Dix. It is probable that in connexion with, or instead of, the usual washing of hands, 'Jesus makes His only change in the absolutely normal procedure of any *chabûrah* supper—one that He

[10] *Shape of the Liturgy*, p. 54.

Himself calls an "example" which they should in future imitate.
Instead of leaving this menial office to the youngest or "the
attendant" whose duty it was, He Himself, their "Master and
Lord" takes the customary towel and basin, and with heart-
breaking humility washes not their hands but their feet.'
Then after His well-known conversation with Peter 'He
reclines once more upon the "first couch", and the talk
continues'.[11] Possibly it was then that the conversations and
discourses of Jesus recorded by St John took place, but these
discourses, as many modern scholars believe, have become
disarranged, and this makes it difficult to be sure at what time
in the evening, and even where, they were given. There is
good reason to believe that the parable of the vine and the high
priestly prayer of Jesus were spoken on the road to Gethsemane.[12]

'It is growing late; it was already well after sunset when
Judas went out. It is time to end this meeting with the
"Thanksgiving", the invariable long benediction said after all
meals. But tonight because it is a *chabûrah* supper, this is to
be said over the "cup of blessing" standing ready mixed upon
the table. . . .

'On this occasion all is normal. "After supper He took *the*
cup" . . . "And gave thanks and gave it to them." Again the
words of His "Thanksgiving" are not recorded for us. Why
should they be? They were as familiar to every Jew as the
Lord's Prayer is to us. "Let us give thanks", He began. And
when they had intoned their responses, "Blessed art Thou, O
Lord our God", He chanted, "Eternal King, who feedest the
whole world with Thy goodness . . .", and so to the end of
the sonorous phrases they all knew by heart. "And", after the
Thanksgiving, "He gave it to them; and they all drank of it"
(Mark 14[23]) exactly as usual, exactly as every other *chabûrah*
drank of the cup of blessing at the end of its meeting for supper.
And then, when the cup is passing from one to another in
silence, He makes another startling incidental remark: "This
cup is the New Covenant in My Blood. Do this, whenever you

[11] *Shape of the Liturgy*, p. 56.
[12] See *The Spirit and the Bride*, by J. E. Rattenbury.

drink it, for the recalling of Me" (1 Corinthians 11²⁵). . . .

'But this time part, at least, of His new meaning must have been quite shockingly plain to the Apostles at the first hearing of the words. He has just been thanking God in their name in the Thanksgiving over the cup "for *Thy Covenant* which Thou hast sealed in our flesh", and all the tremendous things that meant for the Jew—the very essence of all his religion. And now, whenever this particular *chabûrah* meets again for all time to come—"This cup is the *New* Covenant" sealed "in My Blood. Whenever you drink (the cup of blessing in My *chabûrah*) do so for the re-calling of Me." "And when" like every *chabûrah* at the close of its meeting "they had sung a psalm, they went out" (Mark 14²⁶).'[13]

II

It is unnecessary to make more than a passing allusion to the opinion of some modern scholars that Jesus, on the night on which He was betrayed, had no intention of instituting the sacrament of the Lord's Supper, the devotion of Holy Communion, the Eucharist, which are common titles of the central devotion of the Christian Church.[14]

It is incredible that the Apostles should have practised the 'breaking of the bread' within a few weeks of the Last Supper apart from the authorization of the Lord Himself. Dr Rudolph Otto has shown, I think convincingly, by a careful and learned investigation, that the term 'breaking of the bread' was never used as a description of a Jewish meal, but from the first was used as a distinctive description of the new Christian meal.[15]

Some people tell us they can find no similarity between a choral Eucharist of modern times and the Last Supper. The same objection can be made to the earliest Eucharists of which we have any knowledge in the first and second centuries. Our Lord gave His command to eat and drink in remembrance

[13] *The Shape of the Liturgy*, pp. 57-8.

[14] I shall generally use the name 'Eucharist', because with the exception of the term 'breaking of the bread', which has fallen into disuse, it is the earliest description of this act of worship.

[15] Otto, *The Kingdom of God*, pp. 312ff.

of Him, but He left it to His followers to devise, under the guidance of the Holy Spirit, methods by which the essential command should, as the following chapter will show, be carried out.

For nearly two thousand years, under changing conditions, Christian people have humbly prayed, and still do pray, in substance the words of the English Liturgy: 'Hear us, O merciful Father, we most humbly beseech thee; and grant that we receiving these thy creatures of bread and wine, according to thy Son our Saviour Jesus Christ's holy institution, in remembrance of his death and passion, may be partakers of his most blessed Body and Blood.' I noted earlier that our Lord's words about the bread, 'This is My body', and about the cup of blessing, 'This is the new covenant in my blood', transformed the Jewish meal into the Christian sacrament.

There seems to be a difference of opinion amongst Catholic, or rather Anglo-Catholic, writers as to whether the word 'Eucharist' is the appropriate description of this transformation. A modern Anglo-Catholic, E. L. Mascall, uses this word and claims that the Last Supper was the first Eucharist and was celebrated by the Lord Himself, and criticizes Gregory Dix, who thinks the word Eucharist inappropriate. 'The last supper', says Dix, 'is not a eucharist, for the eucharist is intended to be the response of the redeemed to the Redeemer, the human obedience to a Divine command, the human entrance into understanding of a Divine instruction—"as oft as *ye* shall drink it".'[16] Surely Gregory Dix is historically right in his statement, and a word other than 'Eucharist' should be used to describe the Last Supper itself.

There are no doubt great differences between celebrations of the Lord's Supper and its first institution, but there are no differences in the essential facts. It is therefore necessary to make a careful distinction between the essential and permanent features of the Lord's Supper and those which have only a temporary value. There are elements in the Last Supper which can never be repeated. But the essential facts,

[16] *The Shape of the Liturgy*, p. 77.

words like 'This is my body' and 'This is my blood' (whatever significance may be given to them), and the command to eat and drink, remain for all time and are central in all the varying liturgies of the Church. The broken bread at the beginning of the Supper, and the cup of blessing at the end, must always remain even if the intervening feast dies out, as in point of fact it very soon did. Our Lord's continual presence in His humanity is symbolized and assured by the expressions of 'body' and 'blood'. How can humanity be better described than by the words 'flesh' and 'blood'.

Another essential feature in all eucharistic worship is its corporate character. The *chabûrah* supper, the supper of the community, always remains, and must remain though the *chabûrah* itself no longer exists. When the Anglican Prayer Book insists that there shall be at least three communicants at all celebrations, it preserves the necessary corporate character of the sacrament. The presence of Christ through the symbol of consecrated bread and wine, the corporate character of the devotion which obviously implies fellowship, and the active eating and drinking of the elements (not a gazing or a looking at them), are the essential permanent features of the Eucharist.

Another feature, perhaps not essential but desirable, is the anticipation of a heavenly feast. Jesus refused to drink the wine which He distributed amongst the disciples before the Supper began, because He looked forward to the heavenly feast of the future, a feast which the Apostles expected to share with Him. What this heavenly feast is is difficult for us to understand, but that it is a triumphant festival of joy in the place which the Lord goes to prepare for us we may assert with confidence. Nothing is more significant in the eucharistic hymns of Charles Wesley than his claim of the anticipatory character of the Lord's Supper. Perhaps we may be content to sing with him:

> *Yet onward I haste*
> *To the heavenly feast,*
> *That, that is the fullness; but this is the taste.*

There was much in the Last Supper which was temporary and local, which in the nature of the case could never be repeated. The cross of Calvary, the coming event, cast deep shadows over the upper room. Impending troubles distressed the disciples; the tension of the hour was terrible. The gloom of that night would never be repeated. It was a fact of history which could not recur. So far as the Supper was a symbolic prophecy of Calvary, as it seems to have been, it could not be repeated after the prophecy was fulfilled by the crucifixion.

All the liturgies of the Church have been shaped by the action of Jesus, which may be regarded as a permanent liturgical act. The original action was sevenfold: He took the bread, gave thanks, broke it, and distributed it; similarly the wine—He took the cup, gave thanks and gave it to them. The double thanksgiving for the bread and wine were in early times made a simultaneous action which issued in a fourfold action. It is interesting to note that this formula of taking, blessing, breaking and distributing was repeated by Jesus at Emmaus and by Paul when in danger of shipwreck. The liturgical tradition of the fourfold action is expressed by the offertory, the prayer, the fraction (breaking of bread), and the communion. The importance of all these acts is emphasized in liturgies of very varying character. The fraction in early Christian days was given a high symbolic value; its general disuse in my own denomination will be referred to in a later chapter.[17]

The memorable discourses of Jesus were given for all time, and in the nature of the case could not be repeated. The incident of the feet-washing, relevant as it was to the Supper, was no part of the Supper. The narrative begins with the words, 'After the supper', and although nothing more beautiful and typical of our Lord than this acted parable is to be found, it was in no sense an essential of the Supper. In many Churches it has been, and is, commemorated by annual ritual ceremonies, but it is much more important for Christians to follow the example of Jesus by loving and humble service in daily life and action.

[17] See p. 99, *infra*.

The Eucharist, though always essentially a meal, has become the central act of worship of the Christian Church. Hence there has necessarily been joined to it a variety of devotions, some of penitence and some of gratitude. The hymn sung at the Last Supper has been expressed very richly by music and song in later liturgies. Historical statements and creedal confessions have been added, which, without altering the central structure of the Last Supper, express the human needs and thanksgivings of the Church of Christ in the changed condition of men who realize the facts of redemptive grace as they could not be realized by the Apostles before the redemptive acts had been consummated.

Such additions as have been made were not commands of Jesus to His apostles, but were due to the guidance of the Holy Spirit who continues to teach the people of God. Jesus said: 'I have yet many things to say unto you, but ye cannot bear them now. Howbeit when he, the Spirit of truth, is come, he will guide you into all truth.'[18]

This does not mean that all the changes have been of permanent value. Sometimes they had a local, temporary significance and have been continued though not of really permanent importance; and it must be admitted, too, that it is difficult to believe that the guidance of the Holy Spirit has always been sought or always followed. The written word of God is our final court of appeal, at which human aberrations and misunderstandings must be judged. The chief thing is the preservation of the permanent elements in our Lord's institution, and care must always be taken to avoid the substitution or the over-emphasis of secondary additions to eucharistic worship which may or may not in themselves be valuable. The Church of Christ has lived through dark periods, and days of ignorance and superstition, which have sometimes left their mark upon her liturgies. Where errors have crept into them the work of the reformer is often necessary, and it is always valuable when it is based on the records of the New Testament.

[18] John 16[12-13a].

CHAPTER THREE

The Eucharist in Early Christianity

Come, ye thankful people, come

I

IT IS A notable fact that the breaking of bread is one of the four features of early Christian worship recorded in Acts 2⁴², and that this act is emphasized in verse 46 where we read that the believers 'breaking bread from house to house, did eat their meat with gladness and singleness of heart'. The note of joy was especially emphasized, although the breaking of bread must have brought to their minds the broken and crucified body of their Master. The gladness of their spirit is emphasized by their description of the Lord's Supper as '*eucharistia*' and '*eulogia*': '*eucharistia*' is the Greek word for 'thanksgiving' and '*eulogia*' the Greek word for 'praise'. What a contrast there is between the joy and gladness of the first Eucharists and the sadness of the Last Supper! In the conversations of Jesus with His disciples and in His discourses in the upper room, the sense of impending tragedy is almost unrelieved. Doubtless the thought of the Apostles about the meaning of the broken bread and the cup of wine would be dark and confused although some sense of their prophetic character might not be lacking. It is true that Jesus spoke great and comforting words to His apostles, but the deep comfort of them was only realized in the days that were to come. In the upper room we are mainly conscious of their doubts and fears. Even when Jesus spoke of preparing a place for them in His Father's house, and of the path which He would tread, the words of Thomas, 'Lord, we know not whither thou goest; how can we know the way', almost express resentment. It is evident that the disciples were very confused in mind, especially when Jesus said, 'A little while, and ye shall not see me: and again a little while, and ye shall see me.' What did 'a little while' mean? 'Speak plainly', they pleaded, and when at last they were momentarily satisfied, how they must have shuddered when Jesus replied: 'Behold, the hour cometh, yea, is now come, that ye shall be scattered, every man to his own.'

When people regard the sacrament as a commemoration not so much of Christ as of the Last Supper, and think of it as a memorial service of a dead man, they miss its joy and meaning. The early Church did not think of Jesus as dead, for the simple reason that they knew He was alive, and not only alive, but present in their midst. When they met together in their festal sacrifice of praise and thanksgiving, it was His presence that made the feast. It is difficult for us, who know the sequel of His agony and crucifixion, to enter fully into the experience of men to whom the great redeeming act was only partially revealed in one historical event after another. But the early Christians, after the day of Pentecost, realized the redeeming act in its totality. The Cross of Jesus was very imperfectly understood on the first Good Friday. It was too dark; its meaning was realized, and could only be realized, in the light of Easter morn; not until then did these men begin to see that the Cross was not defeat but victory. But even Easter Day itself brought only the beginning of understanding. Even then the full meaning of Christ's redemptive work was so little realized by the Apostles that Jesus forbade them to witness to Him until the Holy Ghost came upon them. The day of Pentecost was the day of illumination; the power with which they were endued was at least partially the new knowledge that came to them by the effusion of the Holy Ghost; they knew that Jesus had kept His promise and was really, though invisibly, amongst them. It is true, no doubt, that they waited for the future hour of His appearing; but they knew that He was already present, and that though unseen by human eyes, He was just behind the veil, always with them. Moreover, He who had been dead and was alive was not only the dearly loved Jesus of Galilee, but the Lord of creation, the 'Alpha

and Omega'. Their dominant thought about the Christ was
that He had defeated principalities and powers and given to
His people a share in His victory. The inexpressible joy of
this experience was richly felt in the early Church, and a
modern writer, Aulén, has shown how this characterized the
writings of Irenaeus, Christianity's first great theologian.

The difference between the Last Supper and the first
Eucharists is aptly described by Dom Gregory Dix in the following words: 'They did not yet understand, but with Him, by
Him, at the eucharist that uncomprehending *chabûrah* would
become the primitive Jewish Church, which proclaimed from
the first, not His survival of death but "Let all the house of
Israel know assuredly that God hath made that Jesus whom
ye have *crucified*, both *Lord and Christ*". That is an interpretation
of Calvary which they could not have learned from the
resurrection alone, but only from the meaning attached to
Calvary at the Last Supper seen in the light of the resurrection.
The last supper [as we have seen earlier] is not a Eucharist, for
the Eucharist is intended to be the response of the redeemed
to the redeemer, the human obedience to a Divine command,
the human entrance into understanding of a Divine instruction—"as oft as *ye* shall drink it".'[1]

The dominant note of the early Christian feast was joy and
thanksgiving, perhaps one may say thanksgiving even more
than penitence, which expressed itself, as we shall see, with
great emphasis in various ways. It was the presence of the
victorious Christ, realized even when two or three were met
together, that created their joy. For this presence was promised to His disciples in the words: 'Lo, I am with you always
even unto the end of the world.' I know no better expression
of the joy of the early Christians than that recorded by Charles
Wesley in one of his hymns:

> *Thy presence makes the feast;*
> *Now let our spirits feel*
> *The glory not to be expressed,*
> *The joy unspeakable.*

[1] *The Shape of the Liturgy*, pp. 76-7.

With high and heavenly bliss
Thou dost our spirits cheer;
Thy house of banqueting is this,
And Thou hast brought us here.[2]

II

We have no definite description of a eucharistic service between that of St Paul in 1 Corinthians 11, written about A.D. 55, and that of Justin Martyr written about a hundred years later (*circa* A.D. 150) in the defence of Christianity which he made to the Roman Emperor of the day. There must therefore be a conjectural element in any accounts of the sacraments of the intervening period which are largely to be arrived at from varying liturgies of the third century, parts of which obviously preserve early traditions. There are a few reliable facts. The principal one is the continual celebration of the Eucharist. When St Paul wrote to the Corinthians, about twenty-five years after the crucifixion, his account makes it evident that the feast was already a permanent act of the Church and a feature of the missionary churches which he had organized. At the turn of the century, Pliny the Younger, who was then Governor of Bithynia, sent to the Roman Emperor, Trajan, an account of Christian practices in which he refers to a service held before dawn on particular days, almost certainly Sundays. It was probably the weekly eucharistic service. He testifies to the high moral resolutions that the worshippers made, and to a meal that they had in the evening, probably the Agape. In the Epistle of Clement to the Corinthians (A.D. 96) there is a long prayer of thanksgiving which is by many believed to be a ritual prayer then used in the Roman Church with which Clement was associated. The Epistles of Ignatius, written very early in the second century, have references to the Eucharist which show it to have been a recognized devotion, but it is not until we come to the *Apologia* of Justin Martyr that we have a full account of the service, which was plainly regarded already as the traditional central worship of the Christian community. It is difficult to know how far the form of this service

[2] *MHB*, No. 761.

was rigid or extemporaneous. Some light is thrown on the subject by an ancient document, the Didache, the precise date of which is uncertain, though it is obviously very primitive in character, and clearly belongs to the first or second century. It contains evidence of dialogue between minister and people. A number of prayers of thanksgiving, not only for the bread and wine, but for other gifts of God, are said by the president of the assembly, to which the response 'To Thee be the glory' or 'Thine be the glory' is made by the people. One of the prayers, which is of special significance because it is a prayer for the unity of the Church, has been incorporated in other liturgies: 'Even as this bread that is broken was scattered upon the mountains and being gathered together was made one, so let Thy Church be gathered together from the ends of the earth into Thy kingdom.' But it is also evident that extemporaneous prayers were admitted, since liberty is given to the prophets to pray. A special instruction is: 'But suffer the prophets to give thanks as they desire.'

The variety of eucharistic prayers in third-century liturgies shows that there must have been considerable independence in the prayers. The objects of the prayers and thanksgivings are much the same, though there is a variety of expression which may be due to the fact that they were originally extemporaneous or were the written compositions of different presidents at the Eucharist.

It is during this period that the separation of the Agape from the Eucharist seems to have taken place. The Agape may well have continued among the scattered Jewish congregations to whom the *chabûrah* pattern of the Last Supper would be familiar, but the converted pagan population, although many of its members were already Jewish proselytes, as for instance Lydia and Cornelius, would have little understanding of Jewish social meals with their universal accompaniment of Jewish prayers and thanksgivings. It was probably on account of this heathen background that the meal became so disorderly in the Corinthian Church. Instead of contributing individual gifts to a common stock, the richer members feasted on their own meats and wines, and the poorer went away hungry. St Paul realized the scandal of such a feast, and promptly separated the Eucharist from it, advising these riotous people, if they were hungry and thirsty, to eat and drink in their own homes. The separation seems to have taken place very early, so far as we can see from an examination of the writings of Ignatius, Clement, and Justin Martyr.

Unsuccessful attempts to revive the Agape were sometimes made in the early centuries, and in the eighteenth century, the Love-feast, which is the English translation of Agape, was revived by the Moravians and Methodists. Of the Moravian Love-feast, through lack of knowledge, I can say nothing. The Methodist Love-feast preserved the ancient name, but gave it a new content; it rather crudely recalled the ancient meal by the passing round of mugs of cold water and buns or pieces of cake, but in a way that was purely symbolical. The Love-feast has virtually died out in Methodism, although it is observed occasionally. In my youth it was quite frequent, but I always felt as a boy that the ritual of mugs and cake was rather grotesque. Love-feasts, however, played a great part in earlier Methodism; they were meetings for the recital of personal and evangelistic experiences, and often were helpful and profitable. Yet as a revival of the ancient Agape as John Wesley intended it to be, however temporarily profitable in itself, the Methodist Love-feast could hardly be called successful.

The Lord's Supper when separated from the Agape always preserved the form of a meal, though all that was left of the original meal was the bread broken at the beginning and the wine of the new covenant at the end. It was a spiritual meal. The separation of the spiritual meal from the Agape brought out the true meaning as a feeding on the bread of life and as a partaking of His covenanted love in the drinking of the cup of the Lord's Supper.

When we read the account of the Christian Eucharist given by Justin Martyr, we find that the essential features of eucharistic worship are expressed in a mode that we can understand in our own day, for already the service contained all that is essential and familiar in our own celebrations of the Eucharist.

III

There are three chapters, too long to quote here in full, in Justin Martyr's *Apologia*. One of them deals with the first communion of a newly baptized person. After some preliminary prayers, bread and wine were brought to the president of the assembly. When a little water had been mixed with the wine, he gave thanks in a prayer which Justin says is very long. This eucharistic prayer, Dr Gore notes, was probably extempore, as is suggested by the words of another account which described it as uttered with all his might. After the prayer the bread was broken and distributed by the deacons to the congregation, and what was left over was taken to the absent members, especially to the sick. Sometimes it has been argued that this was the reserved sacrament, but it was only reserved in order that it might be distributed to the absent members, who were regarded as a part of the congregation though they were not actually present, and in order that it might thus express 'the dear uniting love that will not let us part'. There is no evidence whatever of the reservation of the sacrament in order that it might be placed in a monstrance for adoration. Justin, however, does remark that this bread is called eucharist, and is not regarded as common bread, since Jesus said of it: 'This is my body.'

In another chapter Justin gives us an account of the ordinary Sunday service of the early Christians. This ordinary Sunday service (except for the Eucharist, which came at the end of it) was a Christianized form of the Jewish synagogue service. It consisted, Justin tells us, of prayers, the reading of extracts from the Old Testament to which were added readings from the 'memoirs of Jesus which are called gospels', and a sermon. It is a curious thing that he makes no reference to psalm- or hymn-singing, though chanting was a feature of the synagogue service, and certainly must, in most places, have been part of the Christian devotions. Pliny, in his rescript to the Emperor Trajan, particularly notes the singing of a hymn as part of Christian liturgy. Readers of *Marius the Epicurean* will remember Walter Pater's beautiful and moving description of a

Christian service a few years later. This records the profound impression made on the devout pagan Marius by the joyous singing of Christian children with its happy 'hallelujahs'. Although this is fiction, it must be remembered that Pater possessed a great knowledge of the period and would hardly have written this account unless singing had been a conspicuous feature of early Christian worship. The earlier service was followed by the Eucharist, in which only the baptized could participate. Rather later accounts of the earlier service inform us that the children, the catechumens, the penitents, and other members of the congregation, to each of which groups sermons seem to have been delivered successively, were dismissed before the Eucharist began.

Probably at this point the offertory was made. The offertory, in early times, consisted of gifts of fruits, vegetables, and other such things, rather than of money. Indeed, Dr Gore says that the services were very similar in character to modern harvest festivals. The people brought with them tokens of their thanksgiving to God for His many mercies. Their sacrifice of praise and thanksgiving was expressed not only verbally but materially, by the gifts which they offered.

The Eucharist was from the earliest times described as a sacrifice. A priest is a man who offers sacrifices, and the offerings of early Christians were priestly offerings, made not by a single man, but by the whole congregation.

Perhaps we may here stress the meaning of the word 'liturgy' as it was conceived by these people. The word has now changed its meaning; in our common use, it signifies devotional forms of prayer and worship. Originally, however, it expressed activity. A man's liturgy was not what he heard or read, but what he did. The thought is expressed by St Paul in a familiar passage; 'I beseech you therefore, brethren, by the mercies of God, that ye present your bodies a living sacrifice, holy, acceptable unto God, which is your reasonable service (*RV* margin—'spiritual worship').[3] This is a priestly action, the offering in sacrifice, not of some dead animal, but of the living personality. St Augustine regarded the

[3] Romans 12[1].

C

offering of the goods of the people as a token offering of themselves.

It is important to realize that liturgy meant action. I remember when I first read *The Shape of the Liturgy* I was deeply impressed by the emphasis that its Anglo-Catholic author placed on eucharistic action, because it called to mind the saying of an eminent Free Church divine, Dr P. T. Forsyth, that the first thing to note about the Lord's Supper was its demand for action: 'Take, eat.' The words of Dom Gregory Dix on this subject are amongst the most forcible to be found in his great book. He emphasizes the difference between modern Anglican worship, and indeed worship in Protestant Churches in general, and that of the primitive Church. 'If you believe that the liturgy is primarily a thing "said", your part in it if you are a layman is chiefly to "hear". . . . "Hearing" is virtually all that we have left to the laity to do.'[4] This is entirely contrary to the practice of the early Church. There, as Gregory Dix says, every man had his own liturgy to perform. The Eucharist was not only the action of an ordained priest, but the corporate action of a whole congregation. The early Church believed and stressed in its eucharistic worship the priesthood of all believers. The contrast between modern eucharistic worship and that of the early Church arises, according to Gregory Dix, from medieval misunderstandings, which have influenced not only the Catholics but the Protestants of Western countries. Liturgy is not seeing and hearing, but acting, and corporate acting.

But let us return to the offertory of the early Church. The gifts were brought up to the altar by the people or by some representatives of them. Amongst the gifts were loaves of bread and wine. One or more of these loaves and flasks of wine were received by the president of the assembly, who blessed, or gave thanks for them, and offered them to God that they might be returned to the people as spiritual food. Thanks were expressed in the Eucharistic prayer, which, as Justin tells us, was sometimes of considerable length. In the early Church this was the only prayer offered at the Eucharist.

[4] *The Shape of the Liturgy*, p. 14.

It was probably modelled on the Jewish prayer which concluded a Jewish feast.[5] The Jewish prayer began, as we have
seen,[6] with a dialogue between the president and the guests,
and it is not impossible that this was the custom in Christianized form in the early Church.

In the liturgy of Hippolytus (A.D. 215), the earliest we know
after Justin Martyr, the *Sursum Corda* is to be found. These
words,

> Lift up your hearts.
> *We lift them up unto the Lord.*
> Let us give thanks unto our Lord God.
> *It is meet and right so to do.*
> It is very meet and right;

are generally to be found in third-century liturgies, and seem
to have been used much earlier. The prayer that followed, as
we learn from the liturgy of Hippolytus, was a prayer of thanksgiving concluding with our Lord's words of institution. The
thanksgivings of this prayer usually included words of adoration, and thanksgivings to God for His creative work, providential guidance, and activity in history, particularly the
history of His chosen people. In some cases the Old Testament
history was recited with great elaboration. In addition, prayer
was made for the whole Church, with special references to
martyrs and saints, and to those who had departed this life in
His faith and fear. The prayer concluded with thanks for the
redemptive work of Christ with special reference to His
institution of the Sacrament. There are many variations in
the details of these prayers, but the pattern of construction is
always very similar. Devotional additions were made to the
prayer when its form became fixed in different parts of the
service and it was often itself sub-divided as in the case of our
own liturgy.

In these ancient services we find, then, the first two actions
of the fourfold shape of the liturgy. The president of the
assembly has taken the offerings of bread and wine, and in the

---

[5] *The Shape of the Liturgy.*
[6] See p. 20, *supra.*

eucharistic prayer has given thanks for them when he offered them to God. It is then that the third action takes place. He breaks the bread. This breaking of the bread—the fraction, as it is called—was regarded as a vital act and a symbol of the broken body of Christ from the earliest times. Gregory Dix, however, is of opinion that its symbolic treatment arose from the thoughts of the early Christians rather than from the intention of Jesus. I cannot help feeling, however, that Otto may well be right in his view that Jesus was thinking of His own body to be broken and mangled in His death.

It seems likely that the thought of crucifixion was in His mind. As we have noted Otto shows that the term 'breaking of bread' was not used of ordinary Jewish meals, but was the title given to the distinctive Christian meal.[7]

In any case, however, the fact that such a symbolic meaning was given to the fraction from earliest time by Christians cannot be ignored. The symbolical interpretation of the fraction was a natural and important fact in Christian worship, which has been observed not only by Catholics, but by Protestants, and by Protestants of the least ritualistic type. His body was broken for us.'[8]

After the breaking of the loaf came the distribution of the broken pieces to the people, who in all ages have obeyed the commandment of Jesus to eat, and thus to feed by faith in their hearts on the bread of life. The service probably concluded, without intervening prayers, with the benediction.

What then was done with the offerings of the people? Sometimes they seem to have been used in the Agape meal later in the day, but from the earliest times gifts were made to sick and needy people. This primitive almsgiving is specially noted by Harnack, and is a custom which has been perpetuated to our own days.[9]

The essential facts of eucharistic worship are plainly seen in the description of Justin Martyr and in all later accounts. As the years rolled on, changing events caused additions to the

[7] See Otto, *Kingdom of God* (E.T., pp. 296-9).
[8] See p. 99, *infra.*
[9] *History of Dogma*, Vol. I.

liturgy. The serious heresies of early centuries made the insertion of creedal statements a necessity. The sense of union of the living with the departed Christians, especially the many martyrs, also influenced the development of the Eucharistic prayer. The realized unworthiness of the followers of Christ caused the insertion of penitential confessions of sin to be added. In the Middle Ages, errors, founded upon misconceptions, crept in. The Reformation made necessary changes, of which the Anglican liturgy gives evidence. But that liturgy, so nobly expressed by the incomparable literary genius of Cranmer, still preserves the essentials of the fourfold action. The Anglican liturgy is also the official form of service of the Methodist people and the form with which these pages will be most concerned.

CHAPTER FOUR

Reformation Doctrines

(A) Memorialism

I

THE STUDY of the development of liturgy from the third century onward is one of great interest. But it is complicated and difficult; satisfactory treatment of it is impossible in a short book. It is partly for this reason that I leap from the third to the sixteenth century, but partly also because consideration of it would divert attention from the Protestant doctrine of Holy Communion with which these pages are principally concerned. I must, however, at this point note that the liturgies of the Greek Church preserved more faithfully the ancient sacrifice of praise and thanksgiving by the offerings of the people than did the Western Church. The part of the laity is more emphasized and the prayer to the Holy Spirit which is called the *Epiclesis*[1] in the consecration of the elements is of special importance. In his earlier liturgy Cranmer adapted it, but unfortunately it was omitted later although Charles Wesley paraphrased it in a familiar verse. It is probable too that the beautiful prayer for purity with which our service begins was of Greek origin, though preserved in an ancient English liturgy (*The Sarum Office*). The English Communion Service, both in construction and content, owes much to the Roman Mass. While there was much in that Service which the Reformers disliked, it nevertheless preserved many important, ancient devotions. Many of the prayers in our Office, such as the collects for the day and other prayers, are translations from the Missal. Some of the Reformers, especially the Continental Reformers, tended to

[1] See p. 79, *infra*.

make a clean sweep of everything bad and good in medieval liturgies. This was not the method of Cranmer, who did his best to preserve everything that was good, whilst dismissing medieval superstitions and emphasizing forgotten truths which the Protestant Reformers brought to light. The relation of the English Liturgy to the Mass makes it imperative for those who wish to understand the liturgy to have some knowledge of the Mass. For this reason I have written a note upon it in the Appendix of this book and also in Chapter Nine have dealt with Mass symbolism. With these necessary preliminary words I proceed to a consideration of the Reformation doctrines.

The joyous experience of the early Church was creative by its sense of the presence of the victorious Christ in its midst. The real presence of Jesus is the essential fact in all eucharistic worship. The revolt of the Reformation had two fundamental characteristics: (*a*) criticism of the medieval doctrine of the real presence, with which we shall deal in Chapter 5, and (*b*) rejection of the medieval abuses of the doctrine of sacrifice and priesthood, with which we shall deal later. The Reformers with one notable exception did not reject the doctrine of the real presence, but did reject the mode in which the Church at that time presented it.

In the popular ceremonies of the Corpus Christi celebrations, the Roman conception of the localized Jesus scandalized many thoughtful people. When the cart containing the monstrance in which the consecrated wafer was shown passed down, shall we say, High Street, people were taught that they could see Christ there and adore Him, and then it would pass down Broad Street and Christ could no longer be seen in High Street. It was like a royal procession, seen now at this point, but no longer at that point. It is true that Romans answered this criticism of the localized presence of Christ by pointing out that this localization took place in innumerable Eucharists all over the world. But this is not a satisfactory answer; for the localization of Christ in the tabernacle in a cathedral seems to imply that He is present in one particular part of the cathedral, and absent from the other parts. While we cannot but reject the Roman doctrine of transubstantiation we may be thankful for the preservation of the doctrine of the real presence however much we object to the Roman definition.

To the question 'What is the Protestant theory?' the only answer is: 'There are many.' Distinction must be made between the Continental and the English Reformation. The Continental was more revolutionary, the English more conservative. On the Continent there were three main doctrines, associated with the names of Luther, Calvin, and Zwingli. Luther and Calvin both believed in the objective presence of Christ—Luther in a bodily presence, Calvin in a spiritual.

The doctrine of Zwingli was purely memorialist. The bread and wine were mere symbols of the sacrificial death of Jesus. The general belief, however, is that the sacrament is much more than that; it is an operative symbol. As Charles Wesley writes:

> *The sign transmits the signified,*
> *The grace is by the means applied.*[2]

Zwingli, however, did not look for any direct blessing from the living Christ in the Sacrament. His doctrine was founded on the belief that the body of Christ is in heaven and not on earth. He taught that it was good for the Church to gather in social fellowship to eat and drink the elements, but he regarded such acts as expression of the Christian's faith in the one sacrifice of Christ on Calvary. It was purely the remembrance of a historical fact brought to mind by the broken bread and the outpoured wine. The Greek word translated 'remembrance'—'Do this in *remembrance* of me'—is *'anamnesis'*. The literal meaning of this word is 'a calling to mind'. Obviously 'remembrance' is a good translation when applied to a past event; but when applied to a present person, such a translation as Dom Gregory Dix gives, 're-calling of me', is better. Sometimes an author, Mascall for instance, uses the Greek word without translating it. There is something to be said for this.

It is not easy, on account of the controversial character of Zwingli's writing, to find a clear account of his doctrine. Some modern writers suggest such a statement as that I have

[2] *Hymns on the Lord's Supper*, No. 71.

recorded is unfair to Zwingli. On this point I rely on the very objective character of Brilioth's book,[3] in which he affirms, notwithstanding the criticisms to which I have referred, that 'It would seem then to be indisputable that Zwingli's teaching on this point is symbolistic, and indeed in an almost defiant way purely symbolistic; . . . Zwingli denies also that the Eucharist can be properly called a means of grace'; Brilioth also says that the symbolistic teaching of Zwingli really repudiated the Lord's Supper as a Sacrament.

It is not unfair to call Zwingli's teaching the doctrine of the Real Absence. This doctrine in one party of the Church of England and in English Nonconformity has been widely followed. An interesting illustration of this is recorded by Mr G. W. E. Russell, who, in reference to his evangelical youthful training, writes: 'I perfectly remember a sermon preached on Sacrament Sunday which ended with such words as these: "I go to yonder Table today, not expecting to meet the Lord, because I know He will not be there." ' His past death was presumably to be called to mind by a reverent act of devotional imagination, but He was not there—He was risen! The communion service has often been regarded as a commemoration of the Last Supper rather than an *anamnesis* of Christ. The violent controversy about receiving the elements sitting or kneeling arose from the Puritan contention that the disciples did not receive the bread and wine kneeling. This is of course true, but what seems to have been forgotten is that Jesus gave no commandments as to how the bread should be eaten and the wine drunk. The methods to be used were clearly left to His followers, and biblical literalists should not forget that our Lord at this very time said: 'I have yet many things to say unto you, but ye cannot bear them now. How be it when he, the Spirit of truth, is come, he will guide you into all truth.'[4] It is an error of anti-ritualists, curiously enough, that they try to imitate long-dead forms.

It is of course true that all eucharistic worship shows forth the Lord's death till He come, but it shows it forth in the light

---

[3] *Eucharistic Faith and Practice: Evangelical and Catholic*, p. 156.
[4] John 16[12-13].

of Easter, not in the darkness of Good Friday. To concentrate one's mind on Calvary as if this were the only factor, if successfully achieved, could only result in a wrong conception of Calvary. It is the victory of Jesus, not the hour and power of darkness, which we meet to celebrate; and not until Easter is the victory manifest, and not until Pentecost were the disciples able to give their triumphant witness to the world. Perhaps nothing illuminates my meaning better than the words of St Paul: 'I have been crucified with Christ; yet I live; and yet no longer I, but Christ liveth in me: and that life which I now live in the flesh I live in faith, the faith which is in the Son of God, who loved me, and gave himself up for me.'[5] It is the living Christ with whom Paul is united, but the Christ who is his life continues nevertheless to be the Christ who was crucified, 'who loved me and gave himself up for me'. But the Christ whom the memorialist thinks of is always the dead Christ. The communion service always becomes for him the memorial service over a dead man. It may tend to become more like a burial service than the celebration of a living and glorified man. E. L. Mascall records that just before Dr Gore wrote his great book on *The Body of Christ*, he had attended at the turn of the century two conferences in which high and low Churchmen met, at one of them in association with certain Nonconformists. The crux of the debates seems to have been whether the body of Christ in the Eucharist was the dead body of Calvary or the glorified body of the risen and ascended Lord. The second of these conferences, which was at Fulham, 'was quite remarkable for the extent to which some of the Evangelical members identified the gift received in Holy Communion with the dead Christ. . . . Thus Mr Nathaniel Dinnock roundly asserted: "The *Res Sacramenti* is not Christ as He now is, but Christ's Body and Blood as separated in sacrificial death for our sins." Dr W. H. Barlow no less emphatically wrote: "With Waterland I understand that the feeding on Christ in the Holy Communion, is on the crucified Christ." '[6] Surely the Christ with whom we have to do is the

[5] Galatians 2[20].
[6] E. L. Mascall, *Corpus Christi*, p. 140.

glorified Christ who said 'I am he that liveth, and was dead'.[7] It is important to realize that it is only by an act of historical imagination that one can think of Christ as being dead, because we know that He is alive, and it must not be forgotten that even when His dead body lay in the tomb He had an appointment to keep that day with a penitent thief in paradise.

Dr Gore, in reference to the memorialist theories, says that the only conclusion he could come to from certain memorialist views is—though God forbid it should be true—that the only presence of Christ in their opinion is that of a corpse.

There are no doubt real values even in this unfortunate memorialist theory. One of the greatest of all hymns was the memorialist hymn written by Dr Isaac Watts for the Lord's Supper. Who can forget the vivid words:

> *See, from His head, His hands, His feet,*
> *Sorrow and love flow mingled down;*
> *Did e'er such love and sorrow meet,*
> *Or thorns compose so rich a crown?*

And the response to this vision is a true reconsecration to Jesus Christ. But is the emotion created by these words any greater or different from that created in the mind of Francis of Assisi when he looked at the crucifix in the little Church at Assisi? The verse of Watts is a very beautiful verbal crucifix, carven of words instead of wood or ivory. Where the memory of Calvary is most effective is almost certainly in the hearts and minds of the people to whom the living Christ is really, though perhaps unconsciously, present. I would not say that there is no value in a crucifix. It conveys to our mind the heroic suffering endured by the greatest of men, and may well inspire sufferers and fighters with evil in their battle, but the crucifix is not the cross as it is seen in the light of Easter.

II

ESCHATOLOGICAL SUPPER

Many scholars, especially in Germany, have emphasized what they call the eschatological aspects of the Last Supper. The

[7] Revelation 1[18].

words of Jesus, that He would not drink of the fruit of the vine until He drank it in the kingdom of God, recorded by all the synoptists, do suggest anticipation of the heavenly feast, anticipation of the final triumph of the Lord. And although St Paul does not quote this saying of the Lord in his account of the Lord's Supper, he does speak of the proclamation by the Eucharist of the Lord's death 'till he come', that is, till the invisible Lord appears and becomes visible, till that time when we may sing

> *With what rapture, with what rapture,*
> *Gaze we on those glorious scars.*

It does not seem that the anticipatory character of the heavenly feast dominated the apostles at the Last Supper. Their minds must have been concentrated on what Jesus meant by calling broken bread His body, and speaking of a new covenant in His blood. But anticipation of the final triumph of Christ must remain a permanent feature of eucharistic worship. One of the writers who emphasize most strongly the eschatological character of the eucharist is Rudolph Otto, whose teaching in his essay, *The Lord's Supper as a Numinous Fact*, seems rather ambiguous in his treatment of the real presence. His sense of real communion with the followers of Christ and their Lord, and with those who have passed on to a higher life, seems to postulate the real presence of the Lord; but in his essay he argues that the real presence to be emphasized is not so much that of the Lord's body as that of the events of Calvary. He feels, and I am sure he is right, that the Eucharist is not 'a "Mass"—that is to say a spectacle, conducted by an individual while the others watch. It is essentially a congregational rite. But as congregational, it is always in every case the festival of the whole *congregatio christiana*. . . . For the supper is the "covenant meal". This covenant is the covenant of God with His people, but for that very reason it is also the covenant of brotherhood of that people within itself. . . . We have to do . . . not with a transubstantiation of a physical substance into a hyperphysical substance but with the transubstantiation of an event (namely the breaking of bread) into another event (namely the event of Golgotha). In a "mystical manner" time is eliminated and what was past becomes "really present".[8] If this event does become present it only becomes so because the crucified is crowned with glory and honour and is really present to make the feast. This is more distinctly put by another eschatologist, C. H. Dodd, when he says: 'He was known to them in the breaking of bread, a sacrament of the very presence of Christ in and with His people. Past, present, and future are indissolubly united in the sacrament.'[9] In his description of what he calls the eschatological meal, he nobly echoes and en-riches the words of Otto: 'In the Eucharist the Church per-petually reconstitutes the crisis in which the Kingdom of God came in history. It never gets beyond this. At each Eucharist we are there—we are in the night in which He was betrayed, at Golgotha, before the empty tomb on Easter day, and in the upper room where He appeared; and we are at the moment of His coming, with angels and archangels and all the company of heaven.'[10]

Dodd does not deny but stresses the real presence of Christ in the Sacrament, and this seems necessary if the experience of Calvary to which Otto and he refer is more than an imagina-tive, though devotional, effort. It is the presence of the living and risen Christ which makes His crucifixion a triumph and not a tragedy. Calvary is there because Jesus, who loved us and gave Himself for us, is there. Perhaps the illustration given by Dr P. T. Forsyth of an oratorio—the substance of which I write from memory—is the most illuminating. The Last Supper, he says, was the rehearsal. Calvary, he suggests, is at once the score and the first performance, and every cele-bration since is a performance, or, as he says, a functioning, of Calvary. Surely if the victory of our Lord on Calvary is to be commemorated it cannot be that we think of a dead Christ, since we know that apart from His resurrection Calvary would have been defeat and not victory. We glory in the living Christ who gave Himself for us.

[8] Otto, *Religious Essays*, pp. 51-2.
[9] *The Apostolic Preaching and its Developments*, p. 234.
[10] Ibid. pp. 234-5.

CHAPTER FIVE

Reformation Doctrines

(B) Holy Communion and the Real Presence

His presence makes the feast

I

THE ANGLICAN Liturgy, which is also the official liturgy of the Methodist Church, expresses graphically the Anglican reform of the Catholic Mass.[1] The two books which I have found the most useful in explaining the Anglican and Methodist doctrine are Dr Gore's *The Body of Christ* and Charles Wesley's *Hymns on the Lord's Supper* associated with and inspired by John Wesley's extract from Dean Brevint's book on the subject. The teaching of these books is almost identical in substance, although the evangelical experience of Charles Wesley adds a rapturous glow to the learned book of Bishop Gore.

I well remember reading Dr Gore's book, *The Body of Christ*, soon after its publication. It was the first book I had ever read on eucharistic worship, and I understood some of it very imperfectly. His emphasis on the humanity of Christ, which is today to me the most conspicuous fact in the Eucharist, I found at that time unintelligible.

I was warned by my friends of the dangers of a book written by this conspicuous high Anglican and recollect my surprise at its Protestant sentiments. I found it to be essentially a book of the Reformation. Transubstantiation was denounced; the abuses of the medieval priesthood and its repeated sacrifices

[1] It is interesting to note that though the Primitive and United Methodists had different sacramental traditions from those of the mother body, liturgical forms were not generally used. But the services, often beautiful in their simplicity, generally showed no disbelief in the real presence.

were dealt with with trenchant protests; strong warning was given against ceremonies in the Church of England of adoration of the reserved sacrament. Dr Gore advised his readers to remember that the Sacrament was a meal, and that its blessings were conveyed to the soul, not by looking at the consecrated wafer, but by eating and drinking; the blessings that our Lord gives in the Sacrament however are not received by the mouth, he says, but by faith. Faith is the medium by which the presence of our Lord is recognized. This too is the Wesleyan doctrine, as the familiar verses of Charles Wesley show:

> *To every* faithful *soul appear*
> *And show Thy real presence here.*

Dr Gore's appeal, as was the Wesleys', was the characteristic Anglican appeal to the fathers of the first three or four centuries of Christian history.

A few months ago, when I re-read this book for the first time, I realized how greatly my thought had been fashioned by it. During the interval I had read fairly widely, if not very deeply, a good many eucharistic books. Most of all, I had studied carefully the teaching of the extract from Dr Brevint's eucharistic work which John Wesley had made and circulated amongst his followers, and I had published a book[2] in 1949 on the 166 hymns of Charles Wesley which had been inspired by Brevint's writing. These hymns were circulated amongst Methodists as the statement of the views of John and Charles Wesley on the Sacrament along with Brevint's book. While the general identity of the doctrine of the two books is asserted, perhaps it ought to be said that Gore's emphasis on the humanity of our Lord is not to be found in Wesley and there is little echo of the happy anticipatory eschatological hymns of Charles Wesley in Dr Gore. Both books, however, repudiate medieval abuses, and both emphasize the true sacrificial character of the Eucharist. In this they are not in accord with the Continental reformers, whose hatred of the sacrifices of the medieval Church resulted in drastic action which Anglicans, although influenced at times by Continental controversialists,

[2] *The Eucharistic Hymns of John and Charles Wesley.*

never entirely followed. Dr Gore and the Wesleys held and expressed the view of the Caroline divines—Lancelot Andrewes, Laud, Brevint, and others.

II

The real presence of Christ is fundamental in the teaching of Dr Gore. Our realization of the presence comes through the receiving of the bread and wine in the Sacrament. The bread and wine—the tokens of the flesh and blood of Christ—are the instruments of our reception of the risen glorified man, Jesus. What is the meaning, Dr Gore asks, of eating the bread and drinking the wine? Some people teach that this is a metaphor of faith, but Gore properly shows that it is the gift which faith receives. There are people who object to the treatment of the sixth chapter of John as connected with the Eucharist, since it was spoken before our Lord's institution of the Sacrament. However this may be, the problem that is faced in that chapter is the problem always to be met with in the Eucharist, of what is meant by feeding on Jesus, the bread of life. Gore clearly shows that our Lord 'directed their attention away from the flesh and blood of His mortal and corruptible body upward to His future glory. "What and if ye shall see the Son of Man ascending where he was before?" He told them that in the ordinary sense human flesh could do them no good ("the flesh profiteth nothing"): that only spirit could impart true life to man, and that the flesh and blood He had been speaking of—the flesh and blood of the Son, ascended and glorified—could impart life to them only because they truly were spirit and life. Thus He lifted their minds to a high and spiritual region, where they could be in no danger of low and carnal misconception. He "diverts them" as Athanasius says, "from a bodily conception". But none the less, He plainly means them to understand that, in some sense, *His manhood is to be imparted to those that believe in Him, and fed upon as a principle of new and eternal life.* . . . Shall we say, then, that by His flesh we understand the spiritual principle or essence of His manhood, as distinguished from its material constituents? and by His blood, according to the deeply-rooted Old Testament idea, the "life thereof"—the human life of Jesus of Nazareth in His glory? Whether these phrases are thought to be satisfactory or no, in some sense it is the manhood which must be meant by the flesh and blood.

'At the same time, it is equally evident that it is only because of the vital unity in which the manhood stands with the divine nature, that it can be "spirit" and "life". It is the humanity of nothing less than the divine person which is to be, in some sense, communicated to us, and not (what would be the worst materialism) a separated flesh and blood. What the Father is spoken of as giving us is the whole Christ—the whole of His indivisible and living self. "As the living Father sent me, and I live because of the Father: so he that eateth me, he also shall live because of me. This is the bread which came down out of heaven." '[3]

The truth is well stated by Dr Westcott: 'The phrase "to eat the flesh of Christ" expresses therefore, as perhaps no other language could express, the great truth that Christians are made partakers of the human nature of their Lord which is united in one person to the divine nature, that He imparts to us now, and that we can receive into our own manhood, something of His manhood.'[4] Thus we read in the consecration prayer of the Anglican Liturgy: 'We, receiving these Thy creatures of bread and wine . . . may be partakers of Thy blessed body and blood'—that is to say, of Thy humanity. The term 'flesh and blood' is perhaps the most popular of all descriptions of human nature. Communion with Christ through sacramental action involves, that is to say, living fellowship with the human Jesus, who, although glorified, is the human Jesus—the Jesus of history—the same yesterday, today, and for ever.

III

While the reformers both in England and abroad rejected the doctrine of transubstantiation, Calvin and Luther both taught the real presence of Christ. Calvin definitely uses the words 'real presence' in the Sacrament of the Lord's Supper.

---

[3] Gore, *The Body of Christ*, pp. 23-6.   [4] Ibid. p. 24, note 2.

D

Though he disliked the ancient liturgy much more than Luther did and devised new forms of eucharistic worship, the real presence of Christ was an essential fact in his theory of Holy Communion. The facet of communion of the Church in Christ shone so brilliantly in his thought that other aspects— the historical aspect for instance—took a very secondary place, but the words in which he writes of the meaning of Holy Communion are beautiful and memorable. 'The Lord in such wise communicates to us his body, that he becomes one with us and we with him. And since he has but one body, in which he gives us all a part, it follows that we through this participation become one body. This unity is symbolized by the bread which is brought forth for the Sacrament; as it is baked out of many small grains, so blended together that one cannot be separated from another, so likewise it happens to us, that we are united and bound together in such a unity of souls that no dissension or quarrel may divide us. . . .[5] Verily we shall have gained a wonderful benefit from Communion, if this thought is thereby impressed and engraved into our souls: that none of our brethren can be insulted, mocked, laughed at, despised, or in any way dishonoured, but that we at the same time insult, mock, laugh at and despise Christ; that we cannot separate ourselves from the brethren without separating ourselves from Christ; and that Christ cannot be loved by us unless we love him in the brethren. . . . Thus it is with reason that Augustine so often calls the Sacrament the bond of love—*caritatis vinculum*. For what stronger incentive could have been used to awaken in us mutual love than that Christ, in giving himself for us, should not merely by his example move us to self-devotion for one another's sake, but should both give himself to be ours in common and make us to be one in himself?'[6]

Calvin violently disagreed with Luther, and was in agreement with Zwingli when he taught that the body of Christ was in heaven. He thought Luther's doctrine crude and foolish, and it seems to be true that Luther's explanation of the ubiquity of Christ was expressed, in a book which Brilioth

[5] 1 Corinthians 10[16-17].
[6] See Brilioth, *Eucharistic Faith and Practice*, pp. 166ff.

tells us nobody thinks of reading, in terms of outdated medieval metaphysics. But the truth is that the doctrines of all three have crude elements in them. Calvin's doctrine that the presence of Christ is spiritual and can only be spiritual, makes us wonder how he could think, that when Jesus visited His people in Communion, He left His glorified body in heaven. To the modern mind this seems crude, and however crude the metaphysics of Luther were, his protest against the localization of Christ, whether in the wafer or heaven, was of great value. Luther and Zwingli were mutually contemptuous of each other's theories, but surely Luther was right when he claimed that local expressions about heaven were metaphorical, and that in reality wherever Christ was, heaven was. It is impossible to talk of heaven—'the bourne from which no traveller returns'—in other than metaphorical language. Some of the early fathers of the Church understood this. The expression 'God's right hand' was termed metaphorical by them, and the saying of St Jerome, quoted by Dr Gore, on the words 'foolish talking' (Ephesians 3[5]) is most significant. Jerome claims that Christians are talking nonsense when they say that 'heaven is curved like an arch, and that a throne is placed in heaven, and that God sits upon it, and that, as if He were a commander or judge, the angels stand round to obey His commands and to be sent on different missions'.[7] It is speaking literal truth, and not using metaphor, when we sing:

> *Thy presence makes my paradise,*
> *And where Thou art is heaven.*

Calvin and Luther, however, were very different men. Calvin was one of the great theological thinkers of all time with an exceptional gift of lucid expression, whose mind dwelt on the majesty and transcendance of God. Luther's religious experience on the other hand was so centred in Christ that Lindsay is probably right when he says that Luther's thinking can be rather called Christology than theology. So Lindsay writes: 'Luther lets us see over and over again that he believed that the only thing worth considering in theology was the

[7] Gore, *Belief in Christ*, pp. 320-1.

divine work of Christ and the experience that we have of it through faith. He did not believe that we have any real knowledge of God outside these limits. . . . In order to know God it is necessary to know Him through the Jesus Christ of history. Hence with Luther, Christ fills the whole sphere of God; "He that hath seen Me hath seen the Father", and conversely, "He that hath not seen Me hath not seen the Father".[8] Luther's tender love for Jesus, his admiration of such words as

> *Jesu, the very thought of Thee*
> *With sweetness fills my breast,*

is very different from the somewhat icy and inhuman spirituality of Calvin, whose followers were in danger of undervaluing the incarnation. Calvin did not think that there was any real difference between his eucharistic doctrine and that of Luther, but he thought Luther expressed the truth of the presence of Christ in a foolish way. It must not, however, be forgotten that in Calvin's latest writing on the presence he approximated more closely to Luther. In the *Traicté* (published in 1541) he 'distinguishes between the "matter and substance" of the Sacrament, which is the Lord himself, and its virtue or effect, and he specially emphasizes that we must really partake of his body and blood, for the reality, according to God's promise, must accompany the sign. Only so is it possible for us to possess the whole Christ, and "in him the whole perfection of the gifts of grace, which we need". Merely to partake of the spirit of Jesus is not enough; "we need to partake also of his manhood".[9]

Luther taught that the whole Christ, the God-man, was present—body, soul, and spirit—in the totality of His nature in the Eucharist. He could not conceive, and surely he was right, of the divided personality of Jesus, and to Luther the second person of the Trinity was always Jesus, the man of Galilee. When he speaks of His body it is of the glorified, resurrected, and ascended body that he speaks. The resurrection of Jesus was not merely the resuscitation of a dead body,

---

[8] *History of the Reformation*, I.473.
[9] Brilioth, *Eucharistic Faith and Practice*, pp. 169-70.

but as it were, of the new created body of His glory. When Roman Catholic authorities claim that the body of Jesus in the Sacrament is identical with that born of the Virgin Mary they quite obviously err. When Jesus at the Last Supper said of the broken pieces of bread, 'This is My body', there was not a single particle of the body of the babe in Bethlehem remaining at that time, and yet we speak of the same Jesus. This also is true of His glorified resurrection body. Of that we do know something. It was capable of passing through closed doors. It was not always recognizable. He appeared in one form to Mary Magdalene and in another to Peter. His body was under the complete control of His spirit as it had not been in His Galilean ministry. What further glory He entered into through His ascension we do not know, but we do know that He is the same Jesus, 'yesterday, today, and for ever'. Whilst present to those who loved Him, He was always invisible, although they looked forward to the day of His appearing.

IV

It is impossible to speak of the presence of Jesus and to evade the facts of its mystery. When Thomas Aquinas gives his definition, he confesses at the end it is mystery.[10] Even Calvin ultimately falls back upon mystery. Charles Wesley's words, in a slightly different context, may be appropriately quoted here:

> *In vain the first-born seraph tries*
> *To sound the depths of love divine;*

or as he plainly states it:

> *Ask the Father's Wisdom how;*
> *Him that did the means ordain!*
> *Angels round our altars bow*
> *To search it out, in vain.*[11]

Though scientific definition of our Lord's presence is virtually impossible, there are certain facts which we can lay hold of,

[10] See page 10, *supra*.
[11] Wesley, *Poetical Works*, III.256, *Hymns on the Lord's Supper*, No. 57.

and none more important than that of the rhyme attributed
to Queen Elizabeth:

> *What his word did make it,*
> *That I believe and take it.*

Archbishop Frederick Temple, after certain sacramental controversies in the Church of England, asserted that her doctrine
was similar to that of Luther's doctrine of consubstantiation.
Dr Gore rather regretted this statement, because of Luther's
ambiguity, but in so far as Luther denied the localization of
Christ in the consecrated wafer, and affirmed His presence,
human and divine, in the Sacrament, there seems little
objection to the archbishop's claim. The presence of Jesus,
Luther says, is in, with, and under the elements—that is,
it is everywhere. Hence the familiar words of Whittier are
true:

> *Warm, sweet, tender, even yet*
> *A present help is He,*
> *And faith has still its Olivet,*
> *And love its Galilee.*

Why, then, seek Him in the Sacrament? The reason is that
this is the trysting-place of Christ and those who love Him.
I know no better nor more beautiful expression of this truth
than a simple hymn of Charles Wesley, which to my mind is
the simplest and sweetest expression and interpretation of
eucharistic experience. All that I really care to say is to be
found in these simple but rapturous verses:

> *Jesus, we thus obey*
> *Thy last and kindest word;*
> *Here, in Thine own appointed way,*
> *We come to meet Thee, Lord.*
>
> *Our hearts we open wide,*
> *To make the Saviour room;*
> *And lo! the Lamb, the Crucified,*
> *The sinner's Friend, is come.*

> *Thy presence makes the feast;*
> *Now let our spirits feel*
> *The glory not to be expressed,*
> *The joy unspeakable.*
>
> *With high and heavenly bliss*
> *Thou dost our spirits cheer;*
> *Thy house of banqueting is this,*
> *And Thou hast brought us here.*
>
> *Now let our souls be fed*
> *With manna from above,*
> *And over us the banner spread*
> *Of everlasting love.*[12]

While I honour the piety and Christian witness of the Quaker poet and of the Society of Friends, I cannot but think that they miss something by neglecting this appointed way, this eucharistic meeting-place, of the Saviour with those who love Him.

I have sometimes wondered whether we give enough thought to what the body of Christ actually is. Scholars point out that the term means more than the word 'flesh', and sometimes may almost be said to mean personality, but wherever we use the term 'body of Christ' it at least includes the meaning of 'flesh', nor must we forget the saying of St John, 'The Word was made flesh', or St Paul's description of our Lord's birth 'in the likeness of sinful flesh'. It is in the figure of flesh and blood in which we find a summary of our Lord's humanity. There have been many attempts by Protestant translators of the Bible to interpret rather than to translate the words of Jesus, which can only mean, when literally translated, 'This is My body'; and words such as 'signify' or 'this means' may well be misleading rather than illuminating interpretations. Surely it is better to translate the words literally and leave their interpretation to those who read them. There is one meaning which can perhaps be given to the term 'This is my body' which is not always given to it. Our Lord's earthly body,

[12] *MHB*, No. 761.

apart from His soul and spirit, could save no one. It was just material, the instrument of His spirit, the material He used in His earthly life for the performance of His mission. Is it not possible that He, really present in our midst, can use material things like bread and wine as He used His material body to fulfil His mission? His body was the instrument of His spirit. Is it not true that the bread and wine are abiding instruments of His spirit for the feeding of the souls of men? The instrumentality of the elements is emphatically and repeatedly taught in the hymns of Charles Wesley, for example:

> *Who explains the wondrous way,*
> *How through these the virtue came?*
> *These the virtue did convey,*
> *Yet still remain the same.*[13]

> *How He did these creatures raise,*
> *And make this bread and wine*
> *Organs to convey His grace*
> *To this poor soul of mine,*
> *I cannot the way descry,*
> *Need not know the mystery;*
> *Only this I know—that I*
> *Was blind, and now I see.*[14]

It is by the reception of these creatures of bread and wine that we become partakers of His humanity, that is, of His body and blood. Our participation in His humanity does not come by gazing upon a consecrated wafer or chalice, or by hearing some person saying the liturgy, but comes by our own liturgy, our own service and obedience when we obey His commands and eat and drink of these symbols of His love which are the instruments whereby He feeds our souls.

v

Dr Gore points out how difficult the language expressing the sacramental idea is to many Englishmen. Like the disciples in the upper room we ask for plain speech. Mystical and sacramental language is often uncongenial. Though Jesus said to

---

[13] Wesley, op. cit. No. 57.   [14] Ibid. No. 59.

His disciples many things which they could not understand, and which only time and succeeding events could interpret, He did also speak plainly. For an understanding of what is meant in such words as 'This is my body' or 'This is my blood' we do well to study St John's account of our Lord's discourses on that memorable last night. Though St John does not give us an account of the Last Supper, he mentions it and gives an account of what happened afterwards. It is difficult to be sure which of these discourses were given in the upper room and which during their journey to Gethsemane. Some scholars think that the parable of the vine was suggested by the cup of the covenant from which Jesus and His disciples drank. It is much more likely that the parable was suggested by one of the vines or by the broken branches of vines burning on the sides of the mount of Olives which Jesus noticed under the light of the Paschal moon as He made His way through the vineyard country to Gethsemane. But a study of this parable re-expresses and explains His words at the Last Supper.

There can be no doubt that words like 'Take, eat, this is my body' or 'Take, drink, this is my blood' were difficult for the disciples to understand. We know that on a former occasion, when He called Himself the bread which came down from heaven to give life to the world, many people left Him. They were not necessarily bad people, but just people who could not understand how a living man, whose brothers and sisters they knew, could be the heavenly manna, the bread of life. Jesus Himself seems not to have been surprised that they forsook Him, or would He have asked Peter 'Will ye also go away?' The apostle's answer seems to suggest the disciples themselves might have done so, except that they knew not whither to go, and realized that there was no teacher like Jesus.

When our Lord said 'I am the true vine, ye are the branches; abide in Me, and I in you', He was using the same sort of mystical language as He used at the supper, language which must have been difficult if not impossible for his disciples to understand. These words have often been interpreted as if they implied absorption, and have been the text of much mystical thinking, but they really imply the unity of the

human Jesus with His human companions, just as eating His
flesh and drinking His blood implied the imparting of His
humanity and their partnership with Him.

What can be simpler or plainer than our Lord's explanation
of this parable? When He bids them abide in His love He is
plainly telling them to abide in Him as He is love. He is not
speaking of the absorption of one soul in another, for any
union with Christ preserves the identity of the person united
with Him. Words like 'in Christ' and 'Christ in us' simply
mean union with Christ, that is, intimate fellowship with Him.
This He expresses with the utmost simplicity when He says,
'Ye are My friends'. Eating the broken bread and drinking
the outpoured wine mean just the same thing, that is to say
communion with one who is about to give His life for them.
How could Jesus better express His unity with His people than
by calling them 'friends'; or by indicating the death which in
the future they would always recall—that utmost gift of
friendship.

Perhaps it seems strange to think that the friendship of Jesus
demands obedience to Him. 'Ye are my friends if ye do
whatsoever I command you.' Friendship, some say, implies
equality, but can that be true of friendship of imperfect men
with the perfect One? We can never get nearer to Christ than
just behind Him. No friendship with Him is conceivable
which is out of harmony with His command: 'Follow Me.'
But He had already shown them that night what His master-
ship meant, when He, like a slave, washed their feet.

Abiding in the love of Jesus necessarily meant 'love one
another'. That is the application that Jesus twice gave to His
friendship for them. There were two specific commands He
gave at this time by which they must respond to His friendship.
The former was to eat and drink of His body and blood and
the latter: 'Love one another.'

The vital importance of this unity between Jesus and His
friends becomes even clearer as we overhear the prayer of
Jesus—the conversation of Jesus with His Father. With what
self-reproach we listen to the deeply moving plea that His
disciples may have the same unity with Him that He has with

the Father. So we sinful and erring men may be lifted up into such a fellowship with our Saviour who is in fellowship with His Father, that we in some sense may become partakers of the divine nature. This, then, is what is meant by Holy Communion, fellowship with the human Jesus through the partaking of His flesh and blood, that is to say, of His humanity. Our fellowship with that humanity, fellowship with His Father and our Father, results in the fellowship of the whole family of God. So Jesus besought His Father 'that the love wherewith Thou hast loved me may be in them and I in them'.[15]

[15] John 17[33].

CHAPTER SIX

What of Sacrifice?

And now, O Father, mindful of the love
That bought us, once for all, on Calvary's tree,
And having with us Him that pleads above,
We here present, we here spread forth to Thee
That only offering perfect in Thine eyes,
The one true, pure, immortal sacrifice.

I

THE REVOLT of the great Protestant Reformers was not, as we have seen, with the exception of Zwingli, levelled at the real presence of Christ, but at the current distortions and abuses of the Mass as a sacrifice. The denunciations of Luther and Calvin of these abuses were almost savage in their character, and not unreasonably so, for even the more temperate language of the Anglican Article XXXI expresses a like indignation. 'The Offering of Christ once made is that perfect redemption, propitiation, and satisfaction, for all the sins of the whole world, both original and actual; and there is none other satisfaction for sin, but that alone. Wherefore the sacrifices of Masses, in the which it was commonly said, that the Priest did offer Christ for the quick and the dead, to have remission of pain or guilt, were blasphemous fables, and dangerous deceits.' Dr Gore says: 'While the sacrifice of the Cross had been offered once for original sin, the sacrifice of the altar was daily offered for actual sins. . . . And again, in the later and deliberate theology of the Roman Church, a view has come to prevail . . . which involves in each Mass in some real sense a re-sacrificing of Christ. . . . Such views as these—whether popular misconceptions or theological errors—'[1] on these were founded the notorious and scandalous actions that so shocked

[1] *The Body of Christ*, pp. 179-81.

our fathers of the Reformation. The private Masses said for the forgiveness of sins or for the remission of purgatorial punishment were made a source of income by a corrupt priesthood. Dr Frere calls attention to these scandalous practices, attacked not only by the Protestant Reformers, but also by the devout Catholics of the time who gave special attention to them, he reminds us, at the Council of Trent. But the whole conception of the priesthood as endowed with magical powers to transform miraculously bread and wine into the physical body of Christ was fundamentally false. The words of the institution by which this change was said to be effective became in their use of them little more than a magical incantation. While the Council of Trent did something to correct the contemporary scandals, its formulas were not successful in removing serious popular errors.[2]

The emphasis of the Reformers that there was only one propitiatory sacrifice, that of the Priest-Victim Himself, one sufficient oblation, sacrifice, and satisfaction for the sins of the whole world, was, and is, completely necessary. This fact is clearly emphasized even by Anglo-Catholic writers such as Drs Frere and Gore and Dom Gregory Dix, as well as by those who hold Low Church or Free Church opinions. It is actually in one of his sacrificial hymns that Charles Wesley proclaims this great Protestant doctrine in no uncertain words:

> *All hail, Redeemer of mankind!*
> *Thy life on Calvary resigned*
> *Did fully once for all atone;*
> *Thy blood hath paid our utmost price,*
> *Thine all-sufficient sacrifice*
> *Remains eternally alone:*
>
> *Angels and men might strive in vain,*
> *They could not add the smallest grain*
> *T' augment Thy death's atoning power.*[3]

[2] See note on Mass, pp. 106-8.
[3] *Hymns on the Lord's Supper*, No. 124, *Poetical Works*, III.308.

The positive object of the great Continental Reformers was to stress the importance of Holy Communion as the central fact of eucharistic worship. This they stressed whilst they emphatically denied any sacrificial significance in the Sacrament. Luther would tolerate nothing that seemed even to suggest any activity or offering on the part of Christian people. He would not even tolerate the offertory, which he said 'stank of oblation'. The compilers of the *Book of Common Prayer* were evidently influenced by such sentiments as this, when even in the 1549 Prayer Book, the most conservative of all Reform prayer books, instructions were given that the money gifts of the people should be placed in poor boxes and not offered at the altar.

It is perhaps rather curious that Luther continued to use the Roman ritual even when he had subtracted from it by his teaching so much of its meaning.[4] Calvin, however, felt that sacrifice was so interwoven in the ancient liturgy that new forms of worship were indispensable.

II

The Anglican Reformers, though influenced at first by their Continental contemporaries, and for a century by English Puritanism, were less drastic in their liturgical alterations than Calvin, and less anti-sacrificial in their theory than Luther. Dr Frere quotes Lancelot Andrewes as saying: 'The Eucharist ever was, and by us is considered, both as a sacrament, and as a sacrifice.'[5] This was the doctrine of the Caroline divines, as the writing of one of them, Dean Brevint, shows in his book entitled *The Christian Sacrament and Sacrifice*. As I have already noted, from Brevint's book John Wesley made an extract under the same title, which he circulated throughout his lifetime amongst his people. To this extract was appended what is even more important, the '166 Eucharistic Hymns' almost certainly written by Charles Wesley, but published under the joint authority of both brothers.

[4] See Brilioth, *Eucharistic Faith and Practice*, p. 110.
[5] *The Anaphora*, p. 24.

Though the Anglican Reformers, like Luther and Calvin, have generally regarded Holy Communion as the central reality of the Eucharist, we can never forget that the name 'Sacrifice' was given to this devotion from the very earliest time. Can anything be more admirable than those early sacrifices of praise and thanksgiving (*eulogia* and *eucharistia*), which as we have already seen[6] expressed the joy and gratitude of early Christians, and expressed it not only in hymns and prayers, but in actual gifts?

Perhaps the central struggle between the High Church and Puritan parties of the Church of England is best symbolized by the two words 'altar' and 'table'. The Puritan and Continental Protestant objection to the term 'altar' was due to their detestation of anything that suggested its use for propitiatory sacrifices by the priests and also to the fact that the lower part of the altar was a reliquary in which the bones of saints were often preserved and venerated. Protestants naturally feared the superstitious invocation of the saints which they associated with the altar. They were successful in dislodging the altar from its original place, and in replacing it for some years by communion tables in the naves of the churches. The four-legged communion table is perhaps the most vivid symbol of left-wing Protestantism.[7]

The Caroline divines, headed by Archbishop Laud, reinstated the altars, and by Laud's instructions, railed them in in the chancels where they originally stood, till in 1661 the Anglican tradition became dominant, and the Puritans worshipped in their own meeting-houses and chapels. Even to this day the term 'altar' is often disliked and even denounced by many evangelical Christians, both of the Anglican communion and of the Free Churches. Although the Wesleyans in many ways were Puritans, it is an interesting fact that their sacramental beliefs and practices in Wesley's lifetime were those of the Caroline divines.

The word 'altar' is to be found in Charles Wesley's hymns. The following verse is an interesting instance:

[6] See p. 26, *supra.*   [7] See Chap. 9, *infra.*

Angels in fix'd amazement
Around our altars hover,
    With eager gaze
    Adore the grace
Of our eternal Lover.[8]

Though Anglicans generally shared the Continental repudiation of medieval abuses and errors, there was at least a persistent body amongst them who clung to eucharistic sacrifice. In what sense then can we who repudiate the medieval abuses of this term legitimately use the descriptive word 'sacrifice'? There are those today who contend that when we celebrate Holy Communion we go not to give but to receive. This of course is true so far as the sacrifice of Christ is all-sufficient and needs no propitiatory addition to it. But is it true in a wider sense? Is there no such thing as a sacrifice of praise and thanksgiving? Does not our response of gratitude to God for His creative and redemptive mercies express itself truly in the sacrifice and consecration of ourselves?

III

There are three ways in which we can use the word 'sacrifice' as descriptive of Protestant worship:
- (*a*) A commemorative sacrifice.
- (*b*) A sacrifice of praise and thanksgiving.
- (*c*) The sacrifice of consecrated personalities.

(*a*) *A commemorative sacrifice*

It is the one perfect, sufficient sacrifice of Jesus Christ which is commemorated, and is commemorated by the sacramental action. The broken and distributed bread and the wine outpoured recall perpetually the crucifixion of Christ of which bread and wine were prophetic symbols. So Charles Wesley wrote:

[8] Op. cit. No. 162. It is interesting to note that this hymn is published in the revised edition of *Hymns Ancient and Modern*, but is omitted from the *Methodist Hymn-book*.

With solemn faith we offer up,
  And spread before Thy glorious eyes,
That only ground of all our hope,
  That precious, bleeding sacrifice.[9]

The risen, glorified Christ is really present at the feast.
Indeed, 'His presence makes the feast'. But at all times we
recall His passion and death, seen and realized by us in the
light of His glorious resurrection and ascension. We see Him
'crowned with glory and honour'[10] for the suffering of death
which we show forth and proclaim at every Eucharist till He
come. This is no repetition of Christ's sacrifice[11] as the Roman
Catholics claim it to be, but a recalling of it. It is our plea to
God for the forgiveness of our sins which we make because
Christ died for us. The eucharistic sacrifice is the symbolical
way in which Christians, not only individually but corpor-
ately, plead Christ's sacrifice for the forgiveness of sins. So we
sing:

Nothing in my hand I bring,
Simply to Thy cross I cling.

The scriptural basis of these devotions, both in Charles
Wesley's eucharistic hymns and the arguments of Dr Gore and
other Anglicans of his school is found in certain passages in the
Epistle to the Hebrews and the Book of Revelation. We must
never forget, however, that these vivid and moving words are
necessarily metaphorical. The symbolism is often paradoxical
and not tolerant of logical statement. The description of things
that happen in a localized Heaven is necessarily of an imagina-
tive character. Jesus is represented to us as the High Priest who
has accomplished His work and sat down at the right hand of
God, and also as the Victim which has been sacrificed. The
paradox of one person, both priest and victim, must always be
kept in mind. Indeed the victim is sometimes represented
in Christian devotional theology as acting as priest. One or
two quotations from Wesley's hymns will illustrate what I
mean:

[9] *MHB*, No. 723[2].   [10] Hebrews 2[9].   [11] See note on Mass, pp. 106-8.

E

> *Entered the holy place above,*
> *Covered with meritorious scars,*
> *The tokens of His dying love*
> *Our great High-priest in glory bears;*
> *He pleads His passion on the tree,*
> *He shows Himself to God for me.*[12]

A priest with meritorious scars is both Priest and Victim. This appears even more clearly in another hymn. The High Priest is described:

> *He ever lives above,*
> *For me to intercede,*
> *His all redeeming love,*
> *His precious blood, to plead;*
> *His blood atoned for all our race,*
> *And sprinkles now the throne of grace.*[13]

But it is the Victim who seems to do the intercessory work of the High Priest.

> *Five bleeding wounds He bears,*
> *Received on Calvary;*
> *They pour effectual prayers,*
> *They strongly speak for me:*
> *Forgive him, O forgive! they cry,*
> *Nor let that ransomed sinner die!*[14]

It is interesting to note that in the Epistle to the Hebrews the author thinks of the passion and death of Christ as a past event which the High Priest, the Victim of Calvary, continually pleads, since, as we read in St Paul: 'He ever lives to make intercession for us.'[15] There is a sense in which the Eucharist is, as it were, a replica of the intercession of Christ in heaven.

> *We sing our songs in hymns below,*
> *And they in hymns above.*

Our earthly intercessions echo the heavenly intercessions of our great High Priest.

[12] *MHB*, No. 232[1].
[13] Ibid. No. 368[3].
[14] Ibid. No. 368[3].
[15] Romans 8[34].

(b) A sacrifice of praise and thanksgiving

As we have seen in an earlier chapter, the very name 'Eucharist' means thanksgiving, and it was always called a sacrifice. Not in any sense was the sacrifice of Calvary repeated, but by means of the thanksgivings and offerings by which their gratitude was expressed, early Christians proved the genuineness and depth of their obligation to the grace and mercy of their heavenly Father. The note of thanksgiving is everywhere prominent. It expressed itself in long extempore prayers in which they thanked God for His creative and providential mercies as well as for the redemptive work of Christ which was celebrated by the broken bread and poured-out wine. The genuineness of the thanksgiving was confirmed by the gifts which they offered at the altar, from which was taken, by the president of the assembly, the bread consecrated to God and broken as a symbol of redeeming grace. No sense whatever of any propitiatory or supplementary sacrifice to that of Christ was in their minds, but gratitude and thankfulness inspired their offerings and sacrifices of love. But these were more than mere gifts. They indicated the sacrifice of their person to the service of God. 'St Augustine said to his people at their first Communion: "There you are, upon the table; there you are, in the Chalice. If you have received well; you are what you have received." '

The offertory, it will be remembered, was particularly objectionable to Luther, who saw in it the danger of oblations, and felt that it was one of the things that might cause Christians to seek salvation by their own work, rather than by faith in Christ. One need not deny that perils lurk in the offertory as in most other good things, but to express gratitude to God for His mercy by gifts of our goods, especially when they are symbolical of the greater gift of ourselves, is a sacrifice well pleasing to God. There is nothing in our English liturgy, or generally in Western liturgies, which more needs emphasis and re-expression than the offertory.[16] In the Eastern liturgies it has always been more carefully observed. It is important from

[16] See Frere, *The Anaphora*.

many points of view, and in none less than the emphasis it gives to the active part of the layman in eucharistic worship. The most important protection against the abuses of the priesthood which Luther so rightly abominated is to be found in the activity of all believers; the fact of the priesthood of all believers and the importance of their corporate activity may only be slightly expressed by the ancient offertory, but anything that emphasizes the fact that the celebrant in eucharistic worship is only the representative of the people, who are the real priesthood making their offerings to God, is of vital importance.[17]

(c) *The greatest offering is the gift of ourselves*

The quotation from St Augustine shows how the great fact of sacrifice—the meaning of the offering of our goods—is the gift of ourselves of which they are the tokens. In the Anglican Office the sacrifice of ourselves is expressed by the prayer after communion, which may be called our personal response to God's mercy. In this prayer we find treasured the sacrificial truths which the Anglican fathers have preserved from earlier liturgies. The true sacrificial meaning of the Eucharist and our obligation in self-offering surely has never found more moving and compulsive expression. Here the ancient formula of the 'sacrifice of praise and thanksgiving' finds its true implementation in the sacrifice of ourselves, which is our reasonable service, that is to say, our reasonable liturgy. But so we pray: 'O Lord and heavenly Father, we thy humble servants entirely desire thy fatherly goodness mercifully to accept this our sacrifice of praise and thanksgiving; most humbly beseeching thee to grant, that by the merits and death of thy Son Jesus Christ, and through faith in his blood, we and all thy whole Church may obtain remission of our sins, and all other benefits of His passion. And here we offer and present unto thee, O Lord, ourselves, our souls and bodies, to be a reasonable, holy, and living sacrifice unto thee; humbly beseeching thee, that all we, who are partakers of this holy Communion, may be fulfilled with thy grace and heavenly benediction. And although we

[17] See note on Mass, pp. 106-8, *infra.*

be unworthy, through our manifold sins, to offer unto thee any sacrifice, yet we beseech thee to accept this our bounden duty and service; not weighing our merits, but pardoning our offences.'

There are some who think that this beautiful prayer would be better placed with the Lord's prayer—the sum of all prayers —following it, before the distribution of the elements, as is done in the Prayer Book of 1549 and in the Prayer Books of the Churches derived from Anglicanism—the Scottish Episcopal, the Protestant Episcopal Church of America, and the South African Church. It is interesting that in an alternative service which was composed at the time of Methodist Union for such Methodists as had not been accustomed to liturgies, this prayer was placed before Communion. One reason that makes this desirable is that in our present liturgies it is an alternative to another beautiful and important prayer, neither of which ought ever to be omitted in celebrations of Holy Communion.

Nothing is more nobly expressed in Charles Wesley's hymns than the sacrificial consecration of communicants to God and His service. Can there be any more important application of this devotion than renewed and complete consecration to the Saviour? How nobly this is expressed by two of the consecration hymns of Charles Wesley:

> *Let Him to whom we now belong*
> *His sovereign right assert,*
> *And take up every thankful song*
> *And every loving heart.*

> *Our souls and bodies we resign;*
> *With joy we render Thee*
> *Our all, no longer ours, but Thine*
> *To all eternity.*[18]

It is to be questioned whether in the whole range of English hymnody there is any hymn of consecration equal to Charles Wesley's 'Father, Son and Holy Ghost' from which I quote:

[18] *MHB*, No. 382[1, 4].

Take my soul and body's powers;
  Take my memory, mind, and will,
All my goods, and all my hours,
  All I know, and all I feel,
All I think, or speak, or do;
  Take my heart, but make it new.[19]

Can any better justification be found for describing the Eucharist as a sacrifice than the complete offering and sacrifice of men and women as this hymn expresses it?

It seems desirable to sum up the Reformers' attitude to the doctrine of eucharistic sacrifice. Their repudiation of the term 'altar' arose, as we have seen, from their detestation of the propitiatory sacrifices of the Mass, and also from their dislike of the popular saint worship of the time. The real contribution that the Reformers made to eucharistic worship was an affirmation as well as a protest—the affirmation of Holy Communion. This involved a belief in the real presence of Christ with whom Christians communicated in the meal which brought them into fellowship not only with Him but also with His followers. The symbol of this sacrificial meal was the four-legged table. While we cannot but be thankful both for the stress of Holy Communion and for the protest against medieval superstitions, it should not be forgotten that even in medieval times the altar was also a Communion table and the symbolism was that of a meal. But did not the fear of the Reformers go too far? From the very earliest times the Eucharist was regarded as a sacrifice of praise and thanksgiving and of personal consecration to Christ. Do we gain anything by ignoring the use of a word because of its abuses? At the altar

> *We spread before Thy glorious eyes*
> *That solemn bleeding sacrifice.*

We represent on earth what our great High Priest does for us in heaven.

> *We need not now go up to heaven*
> *To bring the long-sought Saviour down.*
>
> [19] *MHB*, No. 574[4].

So at the altar, which is also the table of the sacramental meal, we offer our sacrifice of praise and thanksgiving and of ourselves, which is our reasonable service. The four-legged table, it may be admitted, was a temporary symbol of great importance, since it is no exaggeration to say that the Protestant Reformation really turned the Roman Mass into the Service of Holy Communion. The Continental reformers especially repudiated the altar, and substituted the Communion table. But the danger of the medieval abuse is not one, as the hymns of Charles Wesley show, that justifies our permanent disuse of the historical word 'altar'.[20]

[20] See p. 105.

CHAPTER SEVEN

Cranmer's Liturgies

THE ANGLICAN Prayer Book is generally acknowledged to be the outstanding liturgy of the Reformation. The Offices of Matins and Evensong were based upon the Roman Breviary, and the Office of Holy Communion on the Roman Missal. The English Reformers strove to preserve all that was good in the ancient liturgies. Archbishop Cranmer was chiefly responsible for the translations and the original contributions to be found in the Prayer Book. The debt which we owe to his liturgical knowledge and wonderful prose must never be forgotten. It is no exaggeration to say that what Shakespeare meant for English verse Cranmer meant for liturgical prose. The rhythm of his sentences and the richness of his vocabulary has made the English Prayer Book one of the world's classics. The continual use for four hundred years of his prayers has never staled their beauty. His sentences have not become threadbare, but remain to this day unsurpassed expressions of the devotions of Christian men. A familiar hymn describes the Bible as a 'golden casket where gems of truth are stored'. These words may be fairly and not irreverently applied to the Prayer Book of Cranmer. While we cannot but be thankful for the literary form and the reverent spirit which created the casket, most of all we are thankful for the saving truths which the casket contains, since for four hundred years English Christians have found in them words expressive of their penitence and creative of faith, hope and love. Of all the Offices of the Prayer Book the Office of Holy Communion may be regarded as the queen. Not only does it preserve ancient devotions and prayers, but it is distinctively English in its character. Without losing true catholicity it gives expression to the contribution that the English mind gives to the Christian religion.

I write as a Methodist, for the Anglican Communion service is the official liturgy of the Methodist Church. Except for a few verbal changes, the Communion Office of 1552 is that which we use today. Although the verbal changes are immaterial, the dropping of some of the rubrics of the Anglican liturgy has been sometimes to our disadvantage, I think, and sometimes to our advantage. Toward the end of the nineteenth century the notification of the manual acts disappeared. Though they have always been observed, and are today, by some of our ministers, the general disuse of them means that the important symbol of the 'Fraction' actually observed in many Protestant Churches is often dropped. On the other hand, the loss of the 'Black Rubric', with its outdated localization of the body of Christ, is an advantage.

Cranmer produced two Prayer Books, one in 1549 and one in 1552. The Communion Service of 1552, with very slight modification, has remained unchanged to this day.[1] The Prayer Book of 1549 was in some respects more conservative than that of 1552. Changes were made in the later work in order to satisfy English Christians who were more influenced by Continental Protestantism than Cranmer himself was. Great efforts (not always, as history shows, successful) were made to preserve uniformity in the English Church. Of these efforts the Prayer Book of 1552 was a conspicuous example. One interesting fact should be observed. There is virtually nothing in the 1552 Prayer Book of Cranmer's translations and original prayers which is not to be found in the 1549 book. Some passages in the earlier book, however, were omitted in the later, and what perhaps is more important is that the prayers were arranged in different order. The ancient eucharistic prayer, closely followed in 1549, was split up into fragments in 1552. But it is a fact worthy of notice that Cranmer's incomparable devotional phraseology, even if to some extent dislocated, was preserved in the later book, and is still prized.

It is important to give some attention to the 1549 Prayer

[1] Cranmer wrote in co-operation with other reformers, but the work is so distinctively his that it is not unfair to describe it as Cranmer's.

Book for several reasons. In shape and order it follows the Roman Mass. Changes made in 1552 are therefore changes from the traditional order which were necessitated by the principles of the Reformers. What were those principles? Two of them were clearly negative: (a) the repudiation by all Protestants of the doctrine of transubstantiation—the localization of our Lord in the wafer; and (b) which is the more important, the repudiation of the repeated propitiatory sacrifices of a corrupt priesthood which roused the indignation of our Protestant fathers. This had resulted in the scandalous commercialization of holy things, so that even at the Council of Trent restatement was necessitated. It is a mistake to think, however, that the reformers had nothing but negative principles. They believed in the real presence of Christ and emphasized, as we have seen earlier,[2] the reality of that presence as fundamental to Holy Communion. Through their communion with Jesus Christ, the Head, Christian men had communion with each other. I must repeat my statement that the reformers turned the sacrifice of the Mass into the Service of Holy Communion. This is illustrated by the title of Cranmer's Office in 1549, 'The Supper of The Lorde and The Holy Communion, commonly called the Masse,' which was altered in 1552 to 'The Order for the Administration of the Lordes Supper, or Holye Communion'.

The Roman Mass in Reformation days, and even now, had become a drama—in many ways a magnificent drama—rich in colour and music and elaborate symbolism, which was enacted by priests;[3] the part of the people was to listen and to look, not to act. Even today you *hear* Mass. What communion there is in it is a privilege of the hierarchy. The part of the people is merely to listen, gaze at the elevated wafer, and adore. The part taken by the laity in the celebrations of early Christians, and even of the Eastern Church, has been entirely lost. The reformers rightly emphasized the fact of the priesthood of all believers. In so far as the Eucharist is a sacrifice, although many of the reformers repudiated that title altogether, it is a sacrifice offered by the whole Church. The

[2] See Chapter 5.   [3] See Chapter 9.

celebrant is never more than the representative of the priesthood of the whole congregation. There was a danger in the violent reaction of the Protestant reformers to the conception of propitiatory sacrifices, that they should ignore the fact that the Eucharist was, and had always been regarded as, at least a sacrifice of praise and thanksgiving. The sacrament is a meal in which by 'receiving these Thy creatures of bread and wine we become partakers of His most precious body and blood'.

The 1552 Order of Holy Communion—our present Office—was gradually evolved. Much discussion took place during the years intervening between 1549 and 1552 between the conservative Anglicans and the extreme left-wing Protestants. Edicts were published denouncing and prohibiting many of the ceremonies of the medieval Church.[4] A comparison of the Office of 1549 with that of 1552 gives us a clear intimation of the changes that were caused by the efforts made for uniformity of worship between ecclesiastical conservatives and radicals. It may therefore be helpful to relate some of these changes. In the 1549 Book the pre-communion has only a minor change from that of the ancient rite—the omission of a chant called the Gradual, which was sung between the reading of the Epistle and the Gospel; but in 1552 considerable alterations were made. The ancient Introit was abolished, probably because it was associated with elaborate ceremonial, and simplicity was an ideal of the reformers. An instruction was given that the celebrant should kneel at the north end of the table, on which a white linen cloth was spread, and say there the Lord's Prayer and the Collect for Purity. The object of the reformers seems to have been to emphasize the fact that the celebrant began the service, not as a priest standing before the altar, but as a simple Christian man who said these special prayers—called Table Prayers—for himself. There were two other important changes. The first was the insertion of the decalogue instead of the nine-fold singing of the *Kyrie Eleison* which had been retained in the earlier Book, but the *Kyrie*

[4] See p. 104, *infra.*

was incorporated in the responses to each of the command-ments: 'Lord have mercy upon us, and incline our hearts to keep this law.' The other change was the removal of the *Gloria* which had no logical relation to the pre-communion, to become a fitting climax to the whole service. The insertion of the Ten Commandments was a genuine and typical expression of the English mentality. Moral conduct has generally seemed to English people more important than right thinking.

The offertory followed the communion as it had done in the early Church. The sentences from the Bible, still found in our Prayer Book, were set down in the 1549 rite and have always remained in later liturgies, but it is significant that even in this more conservative liturgy the instruction was given that the money contributed should not be offered at the altar, but should be placed in special boxes and distributed to the poor and needy. It was not till 1661 that the offertory was brought to the altar. When we come to the Communion Service itself, there are notable changes between the two Offices, chiefly in the order of the prayers. Following the ancient custom, the Order of 1549 did not begin with the exhortation to all who truly repent of their sins and the series of prayers which come later, but with the words of the *Sursum Corda:* 'Lift up your hearts.' The ancient dialogue and prayer of thanksgiving and adoration, the Prefaces appropriate to festival days, the General Preface and the *Sanctus* followed, with the addition of the Anthem: 'Blessed is He that cometh in the name of the Lord. Hosannah in the highest.'

After this came the ancient prayer for the Church, but con-siderably condensed. In the 1552 Book the long eucharistic prayer, or series of prayers, was split into fragments, partly on liturgical grounds, but sometimes on theological. The prayer for the Church was placed in 1552 after the Offertory, but with the significant change that it was a prayer for the Church militant here on earth, whereas the 1549 prayer was offered for the whole Church militant and triumphant. The Pro-testant fear of saint worship, and especially of the Virgin Mary, caused the reformers to omit the references to the saints and to departed Christians except for one sentence which they added to the prayer: 'And we also bless thy holy Name for all thy servants departed this life in thy faith and fear; beseeching thee to give us grace so to follow their good examples, that with them we may be partakers of thy heavenly kingdom.' The following are the omitted words of this prayer: 'And especially we commend unto thy merciful goodnes, this congregacion which is here assembled in thy name, to celebrate the commemoracion of the most glorious death of thy sonne: And here we do geue unto thee moste high praise, and heartie thankes, for the wonderful grace and vertue, declared in all thy sainctes, from the begynning of the worlde: And chiefly in the glorious and moste blessed virgin Mary, mother of thy sonne Jesu Christe our Lorde and God, and in the holy Patriarches, Prophets, Apostles and Martyrs, whose examples (o Lorde) and stedfastnes in thy fayth, and kepyng thy holy commaundementes, graunt us to folowe. We commend unto thy mercye (O Lorde) all other thy seruantes, which are departed hence from us, with the signe of faith, and nowe do reste in the slepe of peace, and that, at the day of the generall resurrecion, we and all they which bee of the misticall body of thy sonne, may altogether be set on his right hand, and heare that his most ioyfull voyce: Come unto me, O ye that be blessed of my father, and possesse the kingdom, whiche is prepared for you from the begynning of the worlde.'

In the ancient Church, from earliest times, it was the custom of Christians to recall to memory, by the mention of their names in this prayer, the mother of Jesus, the Apostles, many saints and martyrs (especially those who had been members of their particular congregation), and departed friends. While it is obvious that the abuses of the intercessions to the Virgin and the saints had become so serious that reform was necessary, is it equally obvious that they were justified in their refusal to call the memory of good people to mind and to limit the prayer of the Church to the Church militant on earth? Do we not do well to think of that cloud of witnesses by which we are compassed about? Is communion broken between Christians on earth and not only the saints but their loved ones who have passed behind the veil? This was not the opinion of Charles

Wesley, in whose eucharistic hymns are to be found hymns to be sung at this point of the service, two of which are specially notable:

> *Lift your eyes of faith, and see*
> *Saints and angels join'd in one;*

and the very beautiful hymn:

> *What are these array'd in white,*
> *Brighter than the noon-day sun,*
> *Foremost of the sons of light,*
> *Nearest th' eternal throne?*

The tradition is that this hymn was written in memory of his father and mother. There is one hymn of his, though not among the eucharistic hymns, which expresses in memorable words the oneness of the Church militant and triumphant:

> *One family we dwell in Him,*
> *One Church, above, beneath,*
> *Though now divided by the stream,*
> *The narrow stream of death:*
> *One army of the living God,*
> *To his command we bow;*
> *Part of the host have cross'd the flood,*
> *And part are crossing now.*

After the prayer for the Church comes the prayer of consecration of the elements and the words of Institution, with the rubrical instructions concerning the manual acts to be observed by the celebrant. An important change in the order of this prayer is to be noted.

In the 1549 Book the words are

. . . to celebrate a perpetuall memory of that his precious death, untyll his comming again: Heare us (o merciful father) we besech thee; and with thy holy spirite and worde,

In the 1552 Book the words are:

Command us to continue, a perpetual memory of that his precious death, until his coming again; Hear us, O merciful Father, we most humbly beseech thee; and grant that we

vouchsafe to blesse and sanctifie these thy gyftes, and creatures of bread and wyne, that they maie be unto us the bodye and bloude of thy moste derely beloued sonne Jesus Christ.

receiving these thy creatures of bread and wine, according to thy Son our Saviour Jesus Christ's holy institution, in remembrance of his death and passion, may be partakers of his most blessed Body and Blood.

It is not difficult to see that the extremer Protestants feared that the words 'they maie be unto us the bodye and bloude of thy most derely beloued sonne Jesus Christ' might be interpreted as implying, though this is not necessarily so, the doctrine of transubstantiation. But the omission of the *Epiclesis*— that is, the prayer for the quickening spirit of God—curiously enough, instead of being anti-Roman was pro-Roman. Roman Catholics would not adopt this prayer to the Holy Spirit because they believed that a repetition of the words of Jesus which He spoke at the Last Supper was enough in itself to effect the change in the elements. It is interesting to note that Charles Wesley believed in the *Epiclesis* form and paraphrased it in the words:

> *Come, Holy Ghost, Thine influence shed,*
> *And* real make[5] *the sign;*
> *Thy life infuse into the bread,*
> *Thy power into the wine.*
>
> *Effectual let the tokens prove,*
> *And made, by heavenly art,*
> *Fit channels to convey Thy love*
> *To every faithful heart.*

I conjecture that this hymn may have been sung while the ministers were communicating. The words substituted in 1552 are important because the emphasis is put upon our reception of 'these thy creatures of bread and wine' to the end that we may be partakers of His most precious body and blood, that is, of His humanity.

[5] The archaic use of the word 'realize' in the original makes this alteration necessary.

The words of Institution are followed by the *Anamnesis* (the Greek word for remembrance) as follows; 'Wherfore, O Lorde and heauenly father, accordyng to the Instytucyon of thy derely beloued sonne, our sauiour Jesu Christ, we thy humble seruauntes do celebrate, and make here before thy diuine Maiestie, with these thy holy giftes, the memoryall whyche thy sonne hath wylled us to make, hauyng in remembraunce his blessed passion, mightie resurreccyon, and gloryous ascencion.' The words of the *Anamnesis* are not repeated in the later book, probably because the word 'remembrance' and the reception of 'these thy creatures of bread and wine' sufficiently express the memorial character of the sacramental action.

In the 1552 Order of Service the words of Institution were followed immediately by the eating of the bread and drinking of the wine by the ministers present and by the distribution of the elements to the congregation. This was an innovation. In the '49 Prayer Book, the congregation, after the Institution, responded thankfully by offering themselves to God. The Prayer of Oblation which they then offered and the Lord's Prayer which followed it were in 1552 reversed in order, and placed after communion. The propriety of this change has already been discussed in a previous chapter. When the *Anamnesis*, which is embedded in the prayer of oblation, is extracted from it, the prayer reads as follows (the words italicized are omitted in the later book):

'O Lorde and heauenly father . . . we thy humble seruauntes . . . entierely desiryng thy fatherly goodnes, mercifully to accepte this our Sacrifice of praise and thankes geuing: most humbly beseching thee to graunt, that by the merites and death of thy sonne Jesus Christ, and through faith in his bloud, we and al thy whole church, may obteigne remission of our sinnes, and all other benefites of hys passyon. And here wee offre and present unto thee (O Lorde) oure selfe, our soules, and bodies, to be a reasonable, holy, and liuely sacrifice unto thee: humbly besechyng thee, that whosoeuer shalbee partakers of thys holy Communion, *maye worthely reciue the most precious body and bloude of thy sonne Jesus Christe*: and bee fulfilled with thy grace and heauenly benediccion, *and made one bodye with thy sonne Jesu Christe, that he maye dwell in them, and they in hym.* And although we be unworthy (through our manyfolde synnes) to offre unto thee any Sacryfice: Yet we beseche thee to accepte thys our bounden duetie and service, *and commaunde these our prayers and supplicacions, by the Ministery of the holy Angels, to be brought up into thy holy Tabernacle before the syght of thy dyuine maiestie;* not waiyng our merites, but pardonyng our offences, through Christe our Lorde, by whome, and with whome, in the unitie of the holy Ghost: all honour and glory, be unto thee, O father almightie, world without ende. Amen.'

It was perhaps reasonable to omit from this prayer the words paraphrasing a petition of the Mass about the Angels, but it is difficult to see why the beautiful words about the union of the soul with the Saviour through partaking of the elements were omitted. Whether the reformers thought that the oblation of ourselves added something to the one sacrifice of Christ, I do not know, but their fear of adding anything to His work was perhaps sometimes exaggerated.

The Lord's Prayer concludes, since it is the sum of all prayer, the eucharistic prayers. Then there follow priestly words of benediction, 'Peace be with you', and words which Brilioth calls a form of *Agnus Dei*. These were omitted in 1552, though it is probable that the *Agnus Dei* would be often sung or said.

Now we come in the rite of 1549 to words very familiar to us, words of invitation to those who are going to communicate. The 1552 service begins with them. The 1549 service almost may be said to end with them. It will be seen in the next chapter that the alteration of the position of these words gave a distinctive accentuation to the English Liturgy. They consist of the familiar Exhortation to those who truly repent of their sins and are in charity with their neighbours to draw near to the table of the Lord. They are followed by the Confession and Absolution, and by the Comfortable Words—a really beautiful innovation in eucharistic worship, due, it is thought, to a liturgy written by Archbishop Hermann of Cologne.

F

And these again are followed by Cranmer's exquisite prayer
of Humble Access with its memorable words, 'We are not
worthy to gather up the crumbs under thy table'; 'whose
property is always to have mercy'. The Communion then
takes place, first of the ministers, then of the people, then
follows the prayer which brings back the individual communi-
cant to a sense of corporate worship, for we who are faithful
are members incorporate of the mystical body of Christ. In
the 1552 Book the Prayer of Oblation and the Lord's Prayer
are said after communion, but then follows the noble climax
of the *Gloria in excelcis*.

It is noticeable that several of the hymns traditionally sung at
the Eucharist are omitted in the Office of 1552, and one at
least from that of 1549. The reason for this in some cases is
difficult to discover. Why should the anthem 'Blessed be he
that cometh in the name of the Lord' with its Hosannahs be
rejected? But the omission of the *Introit* is explained by dislike
of the ceremonial associated with it. Desire for simplicity in
this service as has already been affirmed was not the least
valuable feature of Reformed worship. It may be true that
the omission of the *Gradual* between the Epistle and Gospel was
made for the same reason. The ceremony of moving the Bible
and placing it in another position, was, and is still, very elaborate. But generally speaking there seems to have been a
measure of liberty in the matter of sacred song. Probably the
reformers preferred plain-spoken services, but the practical
difficulty of good choirs after the dissolution of the monas-
teries may have influenced them. Choral Communions seem
to have been rare, but there is evidence that they were celebrated by some Cathedral choirs. The Wesleys introduced
hymn-singing, apparently without meeting any objection. In
their great services, unprecedented as far as we have any
information in the number of communicants—sometimes
between a thousand and two thousand of them—it was desirable, in order to maintain the devotion of the people, that
hymns should be sung. Charles Wesley's collection of 166
Eucharistic Hymns was made at the height of the evangelical

revival, and illustrated everything in the Anglican Rite. He seems to have been well acquainted with the 1549 Office, as has already been shown by his hymns for the communion of saints. It is also noticeable that though the *Epiclesis* was dropped in the later Office, Charles Wesley wrote a versified form of it.[6]

The rite of 1549 was one of great beauty and it greatly influenced Archbishop Laud in the liturgy that he wrote for the Scottish Episcopal Church in 1637. As Brilioth says: 'The Scottish rite was a highly interesting document in itself, and it has become the parent of a group of Anglican liturgies, which includes the liturgy of the American Episcopal Church as well as the modern Scottish rite.'[7]

[6] See p. 79, *supra.*
[7] *Eucharistic Faith and Practice*, p. 208.

CHAPTER EIGHT

The Evangelical Sacrament

Come, sinners to the gospel feast,
Let every soul be Jesu's guest.

I

THE CHANGE of the order of the prayers in the 1552 rite, which begins with the exhortation, 'Ye that do truly and earnestly repent of your sins', dominates the whole office. People who are invited to draw near with faith and take this holy sacrament to their comfort are only those who truly repent of their sins and are in love and charity with their neighbours. To be in love and charity with our neighbours gives expression to the words of Jesus in the Lord's Prayer when we are taught to say: 'Forgive us our trespasses as we forgive them that trespass against us.' This is the pre-condition laid down by our Lord for anyone who seeks forgiveness of sins and emphasized by His parable of the unmerciful servant. The people who are invited to Holy Communion are sinners only. They are not invited because they are professing Christians or even good people or because they have been baptized or confirmed, important though these things may be, but because they are penitent sinners.

This liturgy has sometimes been called gloomy, and the difference between it and others, even that of 1549, is striking. Early Christians came with praise and thanksgiving to the supper, and the more usual beginning is 'Lift up your hearts'. Is this a fair criticism? The rite has its joyful and triumphant passages, but it begins like many of the Psalms, in the depths, before it rises to the heights. 'Out of the depths have I cried unto thee, O Lord. Lord, hear my voice'; but the Psalmist crying out from the darkness of night hopes and believes in the

morning, and concludes triumphantly with the words: 'With
the Lord there is mercy, and with him is plenteous redemption. And he shall redeem Israel from all his iniquities.' This
may well be called a song of ascents.

The sacramental feast to which we are invited is for sinners
only. The invitation is graphically expressed in Charles
Wesley's hymns:

> *Sinners, obey the gospel word;*
> *Haste to the supper of my Lord!*
> *Be wise to know your gracious day;*
> *All things are ready, come away!* [1]

The invitation is to all who are penitent. To come without
penitence is to lack the wedding garment.

But is repeated penitence a necessity to Christian men? It is
not difficult to see that men who have deliberately chosen and
followed a dissolute life should, when they come to Christ,
bemoan their wrongdoing, nor has it infrequently happened
that such people, acutely convicted of sin, have, through the
sincerity of their penitence, entered, sometimes ecstatically,
into a joyous experience of salvation. But is it not rather an
extraordinary fact that, except perhaps in the case of St
Augustine, the classical conversions are the experiences of
people whom everybody else thought to be saints. Outstanding examples of this are the conversions of Martin Luther and
John and Charles Wesley. These three men were honoured by
their contemporaries even before their conversion for the
sanctity of their lives. William Law, generally acknowledged
as one of the holiest of men, actually calls himself a 'dead dog,
a stinking carcase'. Such a description of a good man shocks us
when we read it, but

> . . . *they who fain would serve Thee best*
> *Are conscious most of wrong within.*

If John Bunyan is not to be called a saint before his conversion,
he certainly was a good man, striving to live a Christian life.

[1] This hymn is not one of Charles Wesley's 'Hymns on the Lord's Supper',
but its application seems natural.

No more terrible account of conviction of sin is anywhere to be found than in *Grace Abounding*. What are mere peccadilloes to ordinary Christians were regarded by him as sins deserving the fiercest wrath of God. Sometimes the average Christian man feels such expressions as those of Law and Bunyan are unreal and exaggerated, and for him they would be.

When I was a boy, the people in the chapel where I worshipped were fond of singing: 'I the chief of sinners am, but Jesus died for me.' When I joined in the chorus I felt myself a little hypocrite because I could not believe that I was as bad as the prodigal son whose vices had been painted in lurid colours by the preacher in the sermon I had just been hearing, and indeed I had read of all sorts of criminals who seemed worse than myself, and sometimes I had a little doubt whether I was really worse than some of the people in the congregation who were singing this chorus so vociferously. What is the real explanation of this? May it not be found in the words of St Paul, 'They measuring themselves by themselves, and comparing themselves among themselves, are not wise'?[2] The truth is, the saints with the mind fixed on Christ are so humbled by His dazzling light and glory that the difference between them and Him makes them forget to compare themselves with other people, but only to grieve for their unlikeness to their Lord. The explanation is that these men saw their secret sins in the Light of his countenance.

I once visited Chamonix, but through an accident was so lamed that I had to spend the time sitting on a veranda of the hotel where I was staying where for some days I gazed on the shining whiteness of Mont Blanc till my mind and imagination were thrilled with its light and glory. On my return home to England I passed through Paris, which I had always thought of as a bright and attractive city. That day it seemed to me dark and dingy, as it was in comparison with Mont Blanc. The great saint who lives in the dazzling glory of Jesus, the Light of the World, when he looks into his own heart is overwhelmed.

The average Christian man does well to remember that St

[2] 2 Corinthians 10[12].

Paul exhorts him to 'examine himself and so eat of that bread and drink of that cup'.[3] Only one of the exhortations of the Anglican Communion Office to self-examination has been adopted in the Methodist version, and that has been abbreviated. As it will be remembered, it carefully emphasizes this exhortation of the Apostle.

How then should the average Christian approach the table of the Lord? He cannot but realize that it is only the scandalous sinner or great saint who is likely, without hypocrisy, to say: 'I the chief of sinners am.' The one is driven by his outrageous sins to Christ and the other by his vision of Christ is brought to the dust. One needs to live very near to Christ indeed to say such words with sincerity.

I like to think of this service as a series of concentric circles through which one passes one by one to the central table of the Lord. The outer circles are to be found in the pre-communion service, which may be regarded as a series of standards for self-judgement. I noted in the previous chapter the typical English insertion into this Office of the decalogue. Although today we generally use the evangelical commandments of Jesus in the place of it because they comprehend all that it implies, and add the new commandment, 'Love one another', the decalogue remains the ethical standard by which we must measure ourselves. A second standard is suggested by the collect for the sovereign unfortunately omitted from our Office. Although, perhaps, national and political responsibilities could be more appropriately expressed today, it is important in our self-examination to ask how far we have concerned ourselves with civil responsibilities, the discharge of which is the bounden duty of Christian men. A third standard which is set by the Bible, extracts from which are read in the Epistle and Gospel, may make us inquire how far do we study the word of God? Is it a lamp unto our feet? A fourth standard is set by the creed. The duty of right thinking, however uncongenial to the practical English mind, is one which we have no right to evade. The offertory which then follows asks its own questions. I can hardly think that anyone,

[3] 1 Corinthians 2²⁸.

measuring himself by these criteria, can fail to find that he has many sins of commission and omission to give him cause to repent. When the opportunity is not available of using the pre-communion service, such questions may well be privately asked by those who come to the table of the Lord.

II

This penitential attitude gains a new emphasis in the Wesleyan teaching. John Wesley says that the Lord's Supper was a preventing, justifying, and sanctifying ordinance. By this he means that even before conversion a man may find grace at the Lord's Supper. By a justifying ordinance he means what we should call a converting ordinance; but after conversion, through the Lord's Supper, men grow in grace, in sanctification.

Wesley gave great attention to the experiences of the early Methodists. Their experiences helped him to formulate or confirm many of his doctrines. Probably he opened new doors when he claimed that the Sacrament was a converting ordinance. He made the claim because he knew people who had been converted through and at Communion services. Several instances of this are given in his *Journal* and in *The Lives of the Early Methodist Preachers*. Specially notable is that of a woman, probably his own mother, whose epitaph, written by Charles, contains the following words:

> *True daughter of affliction, she,*
> *Inured to pain and mysery,*
> *Mourn'd a long night of grief and fears,*
> *A legal night of seventy years.*
> *The Father then reveal'd his Son,*
> *Him in the broken bread made known:*
> *She knew and felt her sins forgiven*
> *And found the earnest of her heaven.*

Wesley realized that the table ought not to be 'fenced' by ecclesiastical regulations, but that it was open to all people who truly and earnestly repented of their sins. How was it possible, therefore, to exclude from it the unconverted if they were penitent. Although, in his own societies, West Street or

City Road for instance, non-members were not allowed to communicate without permission, all that he demanded was evidence of the sincere penitence of the applicant. He erected no ecclesiastical or denominational fences. A curious story was told of Wesley by Henry Moore, which is possibly somewhat distorted by the rather dull teller. When he was superintendent of the City Road Circuit he found Wesley writing a note of admittance to an applicant whom he thought unworthy of participating in the Sacrament, and he declared that he would not communicate if such a man were admitted. Wesley evidently thought nothing of the accusation that Moore made, but said, according to Moore: 'I would take the Sacrament if the devil himself were there.' 'And so would I, sir,' rejoined Mr Moore, 'but not if you gave him a note of admission.'[4] Whatever this story may imply it shows that Wesley was no rigorous fencer of the holy table. He certainly was not lacking in charity with his neighbours.

It may be claimed, I think, that John Wesley was the real pioneer of the open table. It is the Lord's table, which no ecclesiastical authority has a right to 'fence' except to the impenitent; it is open to all who truly and earnestly repent of their sins. Thomas à Kempis heads his beautiful commentaries on the Lord's Supper by quoting the words of Jesus: 'Come unto me, all ye that labour and are heavy laden, and I will give you rest.' Surely all ministers of the Gospel may say,

> *Come, sinners, to the gospel feast,*
> *Let every soul be Jesu's guest;*
> *Ye need not one be left behind,*
> *For God hath bidden all mankind.*
>
> *Sent by my Lord, on you I call;*
> *The invitation is to all:*
> *Come, all the world; come, sinner, thou!*
> *All things in Christ are ready now.*

I have sometimes thought that the best advice that could be given, at least to some who are seeking Christ, would be:

4 Stevenson, G. J., *City Road Chapel*, p. 376.

'Read the Office of Holy Communion, follow it prayerfully
and thoughtfully, for the way of the penitent to Christ and
His salvation is nowhere better described.'

III

The true way to follow this service is to read it in the spirit of
penitence. I have compared the service to a series of concentric circles. The space between them is to be bridged by those
who penitently seek the realization of the presence and power
of Christ. It may be that some will find another figure more
helpful—the figure of the courts of the Temple, through which
one enters into the holy place, and finally into the Holy of
Holies, from which, because of the high-priestly work of
Christ, no Christian man is excluded.

The devoutly penitent, having examined themselves, rendered their offerings for God's poor, and joined the whole
congregation in their prayer for the Church,[5] now fall on
their knees in response to the appeal to those who truly and
earnestly repent of their sins, and in humble penitence make
confession of them to their heavenly Father. The remembrance
of them is indeed grievous to them. In the Methodist *Book of
Offices* the words 'the burden of them is intolerable' have been
omitted, because it was thought that during the centuries there
had entered into the word 'intolerable' meanings which were
not in the mind of Cranmer when he framed the phrase. But
his meaning was simple and true: the burden of sin is too
heavy for us to carry, and so we cast it on the Lord. By this
confession we pass through the circle of penitence and receive
the assurance of absolution. John Wesley, for reasons not very
clear, turned the form of absolution into a prayer. Since, quite
late in his life, he defended declaratory absolution, and must
have used it himself when celebrating in Anglican churches,
many of us prefer the original form. It is not because we think
that only an ordained priest is capable of pronouncing it, but

[5] Dom Gregory Dix asserts that Cranmer, by removing this prayer from
its traditional context, definitely made it a part of the *synaxis*. The word
'*synaxis*' literally means 'congregation' but is technically applied to the
worship of the whole congregation, that is to say, to what we now call pre-
communion.

because we believe that any Christian man who has experienced the forgiveness of sins has a right to declare to those who comply with the conditions of penitence and faith that their sins are forgiven, even when they have no confident assurance of the fact themselves.

Since many of us say, and need to say, 'I hold thee with a trembling hand', we listen now to the comfortable words of Jesus and His Apostles, so aptly and beautifully spoken at this moment to strengthen our faith in the forgiveness of sins.

These prayers of penitence and absolution occur in the 1549 Prayer Book, but are placed so differently that the change of order gives an entirely new emphasis to the 1552 Office. In the earlier book, and in the Offices of the Scottish Episcopal Church and other Offices which derive from Anglicanism, the prayers are offered immediately before the reception of Holy Communion by men who have already experienced the joy of the Christian life. Before they come to the table of the Lord they speak these prayers in a spirit of humility, ending with the prayer of humble access. The change of the position of these prayers is really revolutionary, and promises the comfort of the Sacrament to people, not because they are good Christians, but because they are penitent men. In the later Office the invitation is to all.

In our Service, our cry to God comes out of the depths; but after the assurance of our heavenly Father's pardon and love, we reach the heights. We come out of the darkness of night into the morning as we respond to the voice which says 'Lift up your hearts' with the happy words: 'We lift them up unto the Lord.' This is a joyous Easter experience.

'You hath he quickened,' St Paul writes, 'who were dead in trespasses and sins.' We know that He hath indeed. And 'hath raised us up together, and made us sit together in heavenly places in Christ Jesus'. From those heavenly places we respond with gratitude to the exhortation, 'Let us give thanks unto our Lord God', by saying: 'It is meet and right so to do.' At this point of the service we are literally using the very words Christians, as we have already seen, have used for nearly two thousand years. This dialogue, as it is called, is the earliest liturgical form known to us and may almost certainly be traced back to apostolic days: and even, as some think, to a Jewish dialogue Christianized by the Early Church. It is found in the earliest liturgy which has survived, that of Hippolytus used in the year A.D. 215 in Rome. The dialogue continues with the prayer of adoration and thanksgiving: 'It is very meet, right, and our bounden duty, that we should at all times, and in all places, give thanks unto thee, O Lord, Holy Father, Almighty, Everlasting God.'

The prayer of thanksgiving and adoration in ancient days was often long and detailed. Grateful and joyous Christians, as we have seen, gave thanks to God for the blessings of creation and preservation, for the history of His goodness to His chosen people, and for the saints, prophets, Apostles and martyrs, especially the saints and martyrs of the Church which was worshipping, and these praises culminated in their gratitude for the redemptive mercies which they specially celebrated in this service. In our Office this thanksgiving is condensed into a few words, though on festival days—Christmas, Easter, and the like—its length is slightly increased by the addition of a special thanksgiving for the day; but the condensation of thought and emotion in the prayer which is a preface to the singing of the angels' song, the *Sanctus*, gains in intensity by what it loses in detail.

The *Preface*, as it is called, and the *Sanctus* that follows it, are spoken from the heavenly places to which we have been raised. We mount up, as it were, to join in the praises of Heaven itself. Charles Wesley calls the Lord's Supper an antepast of Heaven. If we, by our faith, have really risen into the heavenly places, we are able by anticipation to fulfil the exhortation of Wesley to people in trouble:

> *On faith's strong eagle-pinions rise,*
> *And force your passage to the skies,*
> *And scale the mount of God.*

(Is it not possible here to get some glimpse of the glory which he expresses?)

The beatific sight
Shall fill heaven's sounding courts
with praise,
And wide diffuse the golden blaze
Of everlasting light.

'Therefore with Angels and Archangels and all the company of heaven, we laud and magnify thy glorious Name; evermore praising thee, and saying, Holy, holy, holy, Lord God of hosts, heaven and earth are full of thy glory: Glory be to thee, O Lord most high.' It is while we say and sing in these condensed sentences in company with the hosts of Heaven and the angels and archangels that our hearts and minds are most moved to think on the Church triumphant. Here indeed we may find true fellowship with those who have gone before, and say in our hearts:

What are these arrayed in white,
Brighter than the noonday sun?

While we think of saints, Apostles, and martyrs, in that glorious company, we think too of those dear ones whom we have loved and with whom we join our voices in praise and adoration of God. We know little yet of angels and archangels, but we do know the song that they sing, and we join in it: 'Holy, holy, holy, Lord God of hosts.' May we not also sing, 'Blessed is he that cometh in the name of the Lord' and join our Hosannas to the songs of the heavenly host? When Charles Wesley describes the beatific sight which fills heaven's sounding courts with praise, he concludes with the words: 'And silence heightens heaven.' And so in silent awe and reverence we pass through these circles of joyous experience to the central core, the table of the Lord; but before we feed at that table, with awed and lowly spirits we repeat the prayer of humble access, perhaps the greatest legacy left by Thomas Cranmer to the Church on earth. Can any words be fitter for our lips than these memorable sentences? 'We do not presume to come to this thy Table, O merciful Lord, trusting in our own righteousness, but in thy manifold and great mercies. We are not worthy so much as to gather up the crumbs under Thy table. But thou art the same Lord, whose property is always to have mercy: Grant us therefore, gracious Lord, so to eat the flesh of thy dear Son Jesus Christ, and to drink his blood, that our sinful bodies may be made clean by his body, and our souls washed through his most precious blood, and that we may evermore dwell in him, and he in us.'

So we prepare our hearts humbly to wait whilst the minister repeats the solemn words of consecration at the table of the Lord. These words are said, first of all, in obedience to our Lord's command, to recall Him to mind and to glory in the one full, perfect and sufficient sacrifice which He has made for the sins of the whole world. They declare that by our eating and drinking these His creatures of bread and wine we may become partakers of His body and blood, that is to say, of His true humanity; we are united with Him and thus abide in Him and He in us.

The minister at the table is our representative, for we who in Christ are made a holy priesthood are all celebrators of this Sacrament. At this point our obedience to Christ's words is carried out by one man, our representative, as has always been the case. The Lord's command to do this in remembrance of Him, is fulfilled by the celebrant when he repeats the sacred words of institution. His action of handling the bread and breaking it, and pouring out the wine, separates common food that it may carry out the special purposes of our Lord. No change whatever is made to the material substance of the elements, but they have a new value given to them by the fact of their consecration. Our Lord himself is present, indeed His presence makes the feast. As we obey His command He deigns to use these earthly things as instruments whereby His people by receiving them can participate in His blessing. We are dealing here with a great mystery, a mystery that is inevadable even where theologians try to define. We eat the bread and drink the wine with our mouths, but we feed on Christ in our hearts by faith with thanksgiving. Faith is the only faculty that we possess by which we can feed upon Him. Sometimes there is given to us a rich assurance of His grace, but sometimes we feed unmoved. When our emotion is less, it is then that we most need to pray: 'Lord I believe. Help Thou my unbelief.'

First of all the ministers communicate, and during the consecration of the elements and their communion, we either wait in silent prayer or sometimes very appropriately a hymn is sung, such as Charles Wesley's 'Come, Holy Ghost, Thine influence shed', or if a choir be present, the *Agnus Dei*.

After communion, the chief of all prayers, the Lord's Prayer, is said by the congregation. Then, in grateful response to God's love to us we offer ourselves to Him in this Sacrament of praise and thanksgiving, saying: 'Here we offer and present unto thee, O Lord, ourselves, our souls and bodies, to be a reasonable, holy, and living sacrifice unto thee. . . .' I have stated earlier my opinion that this prayer of the sacrifice of ourselves is better placed as the immediate response of the soul to the gifts of Christ before we partake of those gifts. But there is point in making this response after we have partaken of the heavenly food. This prayer of individual consecration should never be omitted. We fail indeed if we make no personal response of the gift of ourselves to Him who has given Himself for us.

One of the reasons I gave for wishing this prayer of oblation were placed before communion rather than after it was the fact that it is regarded in our liturgy as an alternative to another prayer. I see no good reason, however, why both the prayers should not be repeated. The second of them has the valuable effect of making communicants who have been concerned with their personal relations to the Saviour realize the corporate character both of this feast and of the Christian life. It is good to say: 'We are very members incorporate in the mystical body of thy Son, which is the blessed company of all faithful people; and are also heirs through hope of thy everlasting kingdom, by the merits of the most precious death and passion of thy dear Son. And we most humbly beseech thee, O heavenly Father, so to assist us with thy grace, that we may continue in that holy fellowship.' The service concludes with the singing or reciting of the *Gloria*. This song of praise was extracted through the liturgical genius of Thomas Cranmer from the pre-communion in which it had no logical liturgical place. It was exalted to be the climax of the liturgy. There are some that regret the penitential note in it, but in our highest triumphs we most of all glory in the Lamb of God which taketh away the sin of the world. He has a name that is above every name. To the adoration of the Lamb by the elders in heaven,

> *Worthy the Lamb, our hearts reply,*
> *For He was slain for us.*

CHAPTER NINE

Eucharistic Symbolism: Its Uses and Abuses

I

GOD SPEAKS in many ways to His children. 'The heavens declare the glory of God; and the firmament sheweth his handywork. Day unto day uttereth speech, and night unto night sheweth knowledge.'[1] Not only does God speak in His creative works, but directly in the spoken word by the mouth of the prophets. Not only does He speak to the reason, but through and to the imagination. I fear to use the word 'myth', because in English it has become the equivalent of 'falsehood', but the Greek word *muthos* stands for great truths which appeal to the imagination of men. Not only by '*logos*' and '*muthos*', that is by logical and imaginative language, but by music God speaks to many people. For example, Dr Deissmann wrote that no commentator can interpret some of the sublime theology of St Paul. What is needed, he says, is a J. S. Bach.

God speaks symbolically as well as plainly, but the word by which He has spoken most fruitfully to mankind is the Word which was made flesh and dwelt among us. So, we read: 'God, who at sundry times and in divers manners spake in time past unto the fathers by the prophets, hath in these last days spoken unto us by his Son.'[2] Jesus by His life and death revealed to us the heavenly Father, and also by His words expressed to men His Father's will.

How, then, did He speak it? Chiefly by parables or by memorable phrases which were generally figurative and symbolical in character. Sometimes His parables were acted parables—the washing of the disciples' feet is the simplest illustration—a symbol through which He spoke to us in unforgettable language. But 'His last and dearest word', as

[1] Psalm 19[1-2].   [2] Hebrews 1[1-2].

G

Charles Wesley calls it, was the Last Supper. Julicher claims
that this was an acted parable. At least in some sense this is
true, for whatever else it was, it was a prophetic symbol of His
death. It could, perhaps, be better called a parabolic action
than a parable. By a few words He gave a symbolic meaning
to the bread and wine along with the command to His
disciples to eat and drink in remembrance of Him. The
symbols of the Last Supper, bread and wine, contain in them
all that His death and life means for His followers. Their
simplicity makes them a universal language easily understood
by all men. Men have often regretted that no verbal language
is universal, and although attempts have been made to create a
language intelligible to all, they have been unsuccessful. But
no words can convey so well the meaning of Jesus as these
simple symbols of bread and wine. The stark reality of these
universal symbols may sometimes have been overclad by
elaborate ceremonials, but their silent eloquence has never
been entirely smothered. Wherever eucharistic worship is
offered to God, the bread and wine speak of the blood of Christ
shed for us, and of the living bread by which our souls are fed.

The principal witness of the Church to the world is undoubtedly to be found in the devoted lives of Christian men,
but her corporate witness is her worship, and the fact that all
over the world through nearly twenty centuries this symbolic
rite has been celebrated has a significance whose value cannot
be over-estimated. Everywhere and all through the centuries,
various as the forms of liturgy have been, the consecrated bread
has continually said to mankind, 'The risen Christ is here to
feed us with Himself', and the outpoured wine has shown forth
His death for man's redemption.

The Church has often been unfaithful, even her pulpits
have sometimes been strangely silent about the great realities
of salvation; but the bread and wine, though silent, have never
failed to declare them.

II

Supplementary symbolism is not to be found in the eucharistic
worship of the early Church, which, as we have seen, though

joyful, was very simple. Two of the details of the Last Supper, however, seem to have been generally and reverently observed. Justin Martyr refers to the mixing of the water and the wine, a piece of ritual derived from Jewish custom; and the symbolic breaking of the bread, according to Gregory Dix, was widely observed. These observances can hardly be called supplementary symbols. They are still practised among many Protestants, and in some Reformed Churches the fraction is a distinct feature of Holy Communion. John Wesley defended the mixing of water and wine, and some of the eucharistic hymns of Charles Wesley can best be described as hymns of the mixed chalice. In the Methodist Order the rubric as to the breaking of the bread by the celebrant was omitted toward the end of the nineteenth century and unfortunately has never been restored. The practice, however, has been continually observed by a number of our ministers and is really an important symbol the neglect of which cannot be justified.

It was not until the time of Constantine that marked changes in ceremonial and symbolism took place, although the development of various liturgies in the third century may have shown some tendency in that direction. When Christianity became the authorized religion of the Empire, ceremonialism not unnaturally developed. Partly on this account, supplementary symbolisms began to appear. It is also likely that symbolism was helpful in fixing on the memory of illiterate people the historical facts of our Lord's life and death.

Symbolical developments took place in the Greek as well as the Latin communities, but here we shall deal with the Western Liturgy which gradually developed into a dramatic spectacle. Though the Mass was a drama, it will be seen later that it was much more than a drama. Its dramatic character was acknowledged, and indeed asserted, by Roman Catholics themselves. For example, a Catholic writer quoted by Yrjo Hirn claimed that 'just as those . . . who recited tragedies in the theatre, represented to the people by their gestures the strifes of contentious men, so our tragedian, the priest, represents Christ's strife to Christian people in the Church.' Yrjo Hirn further comments: 'It is not merely this dramatic battle that is to be witnessed in the Church's ritual. The Saviour's victory over the powers of evil was prefigured, according to the medieval conception, in the victories which God's people, led by Moses, Joshua, and David, gained over their enemies.'[3]

The gifts of artists, musicians and painters were freely used to enrich the drama. The apses of Churches where the drama was enacted were crowded with pictures of the life and death of Christ. The joy and power of the musician contributed largely. The embroiderer took her part in creating picturesque vestments for the priest. Censers were swung to represent the ascending prayers of the people. All that could appeal to the eye and charm the ear of men and women combined to make this spectacular drama magnificent. Far be it from me to deny that there were many who thought that they were glorifying God by giving to Him the best that art could produce. Princes gave of their wealth, their costly treasures, and other people gave of their skill. It cannot be denied, however, that ceremonialism of this character was in strange contrast with the simplicity of the Last Supper.

If a Protestant for the first time heard Mass, he would be nonplussed by the apparently meaningless movements, gestures and postures of the priest. The relevance of the many censings, the movements of the celebrant, of the vessels on the altar, and of the Bible from this place to that, would undoubtedly puzzle him, and he might not be comforted by knowing that the Catholic laity would also be ignorant of the meaning of much of this ritual. Every gesture, posture, censing, libation, hand-washing, genuflexion, bowing, signing of the Cross, and every change of garments, is explained by Catholic liturgists to have some symbolic or mystical meaning, but there are clear evidences that the meanings, although at some time or other they may have had a significance to the laity, soon became only intelligible to the priests and probably not to many of them. The purpose of these ritual actions seems originally to have been to give (I hope the word is not irreverent) a panto-mimic expression of the passion and death of our Saviour. But although these symbols may at one time have conveyed

[3] *The Sacred Shrine*, pp. 75-6.

meanings to the spectators, the meanings were soon forgotten. The symbols were, however, ritually persisted in after they had become unintelligible.

In the ninth century a remarkable book was written to explain them by Amalarius of Metz. Later liturgists in the twelfth and thirteenth centuries followed this book closely, though with amplification. The symbolism is far from clear. One action is taken to have multiple significances which seem sometimes to have been held together at the same time as explanations of a single action. But it may well be that they were different interpretations given to a particular act at different times after the original meaning had been forgotten. So we extract from the fascinating pages of Yrjo Hirn in his book *The Sacred Shrine* a part of his account of the meaning of these symbols.

'When the celebrant, in full liturgical array and followed by deacons and choir-boys, steps forth from the sacristy toward the altar, he is Christ, who from the womb, i.e. the sacristy, appears upon earth, "like a bridegroom from his bride-chamber". He is also a leader of God's people, clad in ritual panoply, in order that he may carry the Ark of the Covenant through the enemy's country to the promised land. When he stands before the altar with outstretched arms he represents not only the Crucified, but also Moses, who, with his outspread hands, brought Israel victory over the Amalekites; and similarly, according to the ritualistic view, his gestures and movements should recall Joshua's conquests and David's victories.

'. . . As soon as the ceremony has reached the sacrificial moment, the priest's movements, words, and gestures follow the holy action very closely. The celebrant's peculiar, and to the uninitiated meaningless, movements toward and away from the altar, his inclinations of his body and head, his kneeling, and his out-stretched hands—all these movements are in liturgical literature connected with definite scenes in the history of the Passion. He mixes water with the wine in the chalice, because Christ, it is said, diluted the wine at the Communion; he washes his hands in memory of the washing of the Apostles; and he swings the censer three times over the substance of the sacrament, because Mary Magdalene three times—at the houses of Simon the Pharisee and Simon the leper, and at the grave—offered sweet-smelling salves to anoint the Saviour's body. Afterwards, when the priest walks to the middle of the altar, he illustrates the walking of Jesus from the place of the Last Supper to Gethsemane. He prays in front of the altar in a bowed and humble posture to commemorate the prayer that Jesus, bowed and perplexed, prayed on the Mount of Olives; and he sets forth the waking of the disciples when he ceases praying, turns toward the congregation and utters the invocation: "*Orate Fratres.*"

'The great gesture at the culminating point of the ceremony, when the priest lifts the Host and the chalice above his head, serves, in the symbolic interpretation, to illustrate the raising of the Cross.'[4]

At this moment a bell is tinkled. This act, it would seem, is quite natural as a method of calling the attention of the congregation to the culminating act of the elevation of the host. The symbolical interpretations of the tinkling bell illustrate the absurdities to which symbolism can reach. Here are two illustrations of its alleged mystical significance. We are to recall, the ritualists say, at the ringing of the bell, the blare of the trumpets with which the Roman soldiers were wont to drown the cries of the criminals and the murmurs of the spectators at executions. If this does not satisfy us, we may perhaps prefer to recall the great earthquake at the time of the crucifixion.

Perhaps the mystical symbols of the altar are the most remarkable instances of the abuses of ritual symbolism. 'In the Catholic Mass-ceremonial, as interpreted by the old ritualists, the lifeless objects on the altar, the chalice, the paten, and even the altar-cloth, possess almost as much importance as the living person. The holy cup, for example, is not only the vessel in which the wine is transformed into a eucharistic divinity, but it also corresponds to the chamber in which the Divine Man was hidden when dead. When the priest has

4 *The Sacred Shrine*, pp. 75ff.

dipped a portion of the Host in the chalice after the consecration, it is said that he has therewith buried Christ anew; and
when later the paten is placed over the mouth of the chalice,
the stone has herewith been rolled to the entrance of the grave.
The little piece of cloth, which covers the chalice when it is
lifted from the altar, represents the winding sheet in which the
body was taken down from the Cross. Again, the cloth which
is spread upon the altar, for the consecrated wafer or for a
fragment of it to rest upon, is the winding sheet that covered
the Saviour in His grave; but it can also, and especially at
Christmas Masses, be regarded as the swaddling-cloth in which
the new-born Babe was wrapped.'[5] Can symbolism reach
deeper depths than these last alternatives imply? It is difficult
to think that the same cloth can both symbolize the winding
sheet of the dead and the swaddling clothes of a baby.

I would not suggest that these supplementary symbolisms
have had no value. It may well be that visual objects would
help illiterate people to recollect the historical facts of the
Passion. A devout priest, when celebrating might be able, as
he pondered upon the symbolic significance of his gestures and
postures to concentrate his attention on the great events of the
Redeemer's work. But it is difficult to justify the repetition of
a symbol when its meaning has been forgotten. Symbols are
useful to everybody. Many of us learnt the alphabet by means
of symbolic pictures; 'A', we were reminded, was an 'Archer',
and the picture of him with his bow and arrow may have
helped us in the learning of the alphabet. But when we have
accomplished our task we forget the symbol. If we followed
the method of medieval symbolism we should preserve the
picture of the archer with his bow as a precious relic, and
perhaps give to it a new interpretation. It would symbolize
the battle of Agincourt and the triumph of English bowmen
over the French. But when the symbol is no longer of use to
us, we do not perpetuate it. The use of symbols of this sort is
temporary. Their continuation because they were once useful
is surely grotesque.

An additional weakness of these supplementary symbols is

[5] Ibid., pp. 79-80.

that they tend to divert attention from the primary one. Men's minds become interested in secondary things, so that their attention is fixed rather on the priest and his actions than upon his Lord. This indeed became, through the ceremonialism in which the priest was the central figure, the most disastrous evil of ritual ceremonialism. Can we wonder that at the Reformation many ceremonies were ruthlessly abandoned? Between 1549 and 1552, when the Prayer Book was being revised, a holocaust of Catholic ceremonies was made by the edicts of Parliament, a list of which may be recited.

Between 1549 and 1552 'certain Articles were issued to the clergy, prohibiting the use of various ceremonies in the Mass. The following are specified: "Kissing the Lord's Table; washing the fingers; blessing His eyes with patten or sudary; crossing His head with the patten; shifting of the book from one place to another; laying down and licking the chalice; holding up His fingers, hands, or thumbs; breathing upon the bread or chalice; showing the Sacrament openly before the distribution of the Communion; ringing of sacrying bells; setting any light upon the Lord's Board at any time; and finally, to use no other ceremonies than are appointed in the King's Book of Common Prayers.'[6]

III

The Mass was much more than drama, and the priests were no mere actors on a theatrical stage. They were performing what they thought to be a miracle, the miracle which by the recital of the Lord's words of institution changed the bread and wine into the body and blood of our Saviour. Although it is true that the supplementary symbols of the Mass were generally symbols of Christ and His passion and death, the great act of the Mass was the action of the priests as they performed their miracle, and since by that miracle men believed that their daily sins were forgiven, the thoughts of the spectators must have been concentrated on the priests. They undoubtedly believed that Jesus had suffered and died for the sins of the whole world, but that happened a long time before.

[6] Lathbury, *Book of Common Prayer*, p. 31.

Here and now, however, His body and blood were really present, they thought, in the transubstantiated bread and wine. But for all this, as Catholic authorities themselves say, the bread and wine (however much more they were) were symbols.[7]

The Reformers of the sixteenth century repudiated propitiatory sacrifices, and did away with the altar as the symbol of them, getting rid at the same time of its use as a reliquary, and retained its use as the table of the Lord's Supper only. But the Reformers, with all their dislike of Catholic symbolism could not escape from symbols. So they created a new one— the four-legged table. It was clearly impossible that such a table should be used as a reliquary and provide a covering for the bones of dead saints.

The time will never come when men and women, especially in their collective gatherings, can do without symbols. How far the supplementary eucharistic symbols are valuable is a matter on which opinions differ, but when in any way they obscure the Lord's simple and universal symbols of bread and wine, and His invitation to all penitent men and women to come to the feast which His presence makes, they are mischievous.

[7] See Appendix, pp. 106-8, *infra.*

Roman Mass

A MODERN Roman Catholic writer[1] quotes the Council of Trent on the sacrifice of the Mass in the following words: 'At the last Supper, on the night on which He was betrayed, in order that He might leave the Church, His well-beloved spouse, a visible sacrifice demanded by human nature, a sacrifice, too, which would represent and recall to the end of time the bloody immolation about to be accomplished once for all on the Cross, and which would apply to us the saving power of this immolation for the remission of our daily sins, Jesus declared Himself the Priest established for ever according to the order of Melchisedech. As such He offered to God His Body and His Blood under the species of bread and wine. And under the appearances of the same elements He gave them to the Apostles to take. Those Apostles He then constituted priests of the New Testament, and by these words, "Do this in commemoration of Me", He ordered them and their successors in the priesthood to perform that oblation: thus has the Catholic Church always understood and taught.'

The Roman priests believe that by pronouncing certain words they can actually transform bread and wine into the body of Christ, and then offer this body to God in sacrifice. Whilst they claim that our Lord's sacrifice of Himself is the one sufficient sacrifice—the only bloody sacrifice—they also claim that when Jesus said to His apostles, 'Do this', He empowered them and all their successors—that is, the ordained priesthood of the Church—to do what He did at the Last Supper. It is often said by Protestants that Catholics believe the Mass to be a repetition of the sacrifice of Calvary. It is

[1] Pierre Maranget.

only fair to point out that this is not exactly what the Catholics say. Their claim is that the Mass is a repetition of the Last Supper, but with certain differences that arise from the fact that the Last Supper contemplated the future event of the Crucifixion. The Last Supper, they say, was a prophetic offering; the Mass is a memorial offering of the body and blood of Christ. But the value or valuelessness of this theory depends on the interpretation that Roman Catholics give to the Last Supper. They claim that Jesus, though there in His bodily presence, by His words and actions transubstantiated the bread and wine so that they became His body, and then offered His own body to God as a sacrifice for the sins of the whole world, and that He commanded His apostles to do this in remembrance of Him, not merely to eat and drink, as the words would naturally seem to mean, but to perform the ceremony of the Supper in its totality again. By giving this command He made them into His priests, and likewise authorized all their successors in the priesthood to make the same offering. At the Mass this offering is made in commemoration of the sacrifice of Christ at Calvary. It is not the sacrifice of Calvary that is made again, but the same sacrifice that was made at the Last Supper that is made again, with the difference that then the crucifixion was in the future and now it is in the past.

The dogmas in this theory have no support whatever in scripture. No one who reads the Gospel accounts could think that Jesus was offering Himself in sacrifice at that time, though by His symbolic actions He indicated the sacrifice that He would make on the Cross. There is no evidence whatever that He ordained the Apostles to a new priesthood, and the transubstantiation of the bread and wine is a theory which was not held by the early Church, but (unfortunately) was formulated in the Middle Ages.

A very large measure of credulity is required to believe that Jesus, when bodily present, transformed the bread and wine into the very body with the lips of which He spoke. That He really meant that the bread and wine was the body born of the Virgin Mary, as John Wesley pointed out in his notes on the

New Testament, seems to all Protestants to be an impossible and even grotesque claim.

While the bread and wine were made by Him the instrument of His Spirit, just as His human body had been, they could not have been but distinguished from the body of Him who spoke these words.

While the bread and wine remain, in a sacramental sense, the body of our Lord—the bread of life whereby He feeds His people—and are given to us for that reason, they seem, obviously enough, different from that human body through which He worked, and which, in a true sense, they represent.

We are fed by the partaking of these sacramental elements, and call to mind through the symbolism of the supper, the offering which our Saviour made on Calvary.

The fundamental fallacy of the Roman theory is that the Last Supper was in any sense a sacrifice offered by Christ to His Father. This is a pure invention. The symbolism, no doubt, of the broken bread and poured-out wine was prophetic of the one perfect, sufficient sacrifice offered on Calvary, but no reader of scriptural narratives alone can find the slightest evidence of the truth of the Roman theory. Nor is there any evidence of the truth of this theory in early Christian eucharistic worship. It seems to have been developed in later centuries in order to justify priestly claims which gradually arose in the Dark Ages. One cannot but rejoice that the great Reformers repudiated so strongly the doctrine of priestly propitiatory sacrifice.